Löffler/Rose/Warner

KU-096-923

Australia

Hutchinson Australia

Photographers:
Adastra, Maseot/Australia Nr. 41
ATC Australian Tourist Commission, Frankfurt
    Nr. 113–116, 120, 121, front cover picture
Courtesy Australian News and Information Bureau 101, 104, 124
Liliane Baumgartner, Bäretswil ZH Nr. 28, 90, 97
H.M. Berney, Montreux Nr. 31, 33, 34, 38, 39, 50, 52,
    56–61, 82, 89, 94
Willi Dolder, Burgau SG Nr. 29, 30, 35, 40, 47, 48
Edgar Haldimann, Lenzburg Nr. 80
Ray Halin, Paris Nr. 6, 8, 11–16, 18, 26, 27, 32, 51, 65, 66, 69,
    70, 72–75, 100, 102, 106–108, 112, 118, 122, 123, 128,
    130, 134, 135, 138 (all pictures made by Leicaflex camera)
Ernst Löffler, Canberra Nr. 1, 2, 9, 23, 24, 36, 37, 44,
    49, 63, 68, 71, 76, 88, 96, 103, 110, 126, 127, 129
Courtesy New South Wales Department of Tourism Nr. 117
Werner Nigg, Zürich Nr. 109
Fritz Prenzel, Neutral Bay Junction/Australia Nr. 3–5,
    7, 10, 17, 19–22, 25, 46, 53–55, 62, 64, 67, 77–79,
    81, 83–87, 91–93, 95, 98, 99, 105, 111, 125, 131–133, 136, 137
Queensland Government Tourist Bureau, Brisbane Nr. 43
Helmut Schumacher, Bochum Nr. 42, 45
Courtesy Van Ewyk Pty. Ltd. Nr. 119

HUTCHINSON GROUP (Australia) Pty Ltd
30–32 Cremorne Street, Richmond, Victoria, 3121

London Melbourne Sydney Auckland Wellington
Johannesburg
and agencies throughout the world

© 1977 Kümmerly + Frey, Geographical Publishers, Berne
    Printed in Switzerland by Kümmerly + Frey
First published 1977
ISBN 0 09 130460 1

All Rights Reserved. No part of this publication may be
reproduced, stored in a retrieval system, or transmitted, in
any form or by any means, electronic, mechanical,
photocopying, recording or otherwise, without the prior
permission of the Publisher.

Contents

Acknowledgements

The authors would like to thank Ms M. Sullivan and Mr C. Margules for critically reading three chapters of the manuscript. Mr Margules also generously helped with the section on Australian fauna. Acknowledgement is also made to the scientific publications used in compiling the book. The main sources are listed below and are recommended for further reading.

Australian National Commission for UNESCO (1973). *Australian Aboriginal Culture.*
Bennett, I.   *The Great Barrier Reef.* Landsdowne, Melbourne, 1971.
Blainey, G.   *Triumph of the Nomads.* Sun Books, Melbourne, 1976.
Blainey, G.   *The Tyranny of Distance.* Sun Books, Melbourne, 1966.
Clark, C.M.H.   *A Short History of Australia.* Melbourne University Press, Melbourne, 1962.
Division of National Mapping, Department of Minerals and Energy (1962–73). *Atlas of Australian Resources.*
Frith, H.J.   *Wildlife Conservation.* Angus and Robertson, Sydney, 1973.
Horne, D.   *The Lucky Country.* Penguin Books Australia, Melbourne, 1974.
Jennings, J.N. and Mabbutt, J.A. (eds). *Landform Studies from Australia and New Guinea.* ANU Press, Canberra, 1967.
Learmonth, N. and Learmonth, A. *Regional Landscapes of Australia.* Angus and Robertson, Sydney, 1971.
Leeper, G.W. (ed.)   *The Australian Environment.* CSIRO, Melbourne, 1970.
Lofgren, M.E.   *Patterns of Life.* A.F. Lovell, Perth, 1975.
Moore, R.M. (ed).   *Australian Grasslands.* ANU Press, Canberra, 1970.
Mulvaney, D.J.   *The Prehistory of Australia.* Penguin Books Australia, Melbourne, 1975.
Ride, W.D.L.   *A Guide to Native Mammals of Australia.* Oxford University Press, Melbourne, 1970.
Rowley, C.D.   *The Destruction of Aboriginal Society.* Pelican Books, London, 1974.
Slatyer, R.O. and Perry, R.A. *Arid Lands of Australia.* ANU Press, Canberra, 1969.
Spate, O.H.K.   *Australia.* Ernest Benn Ltd, London, 1971.
Ward, R.   *Australia.* Horowitz, Sydney, 1965.
Ward, R.   *The Australian Legend.* Oxford University Press, Melbourne, 1966.

Thursday 19th... at 6 saw land extending from NE to West at the distance of 5 or 6 leagues having 80 fathom water a fine sandy bottom we continued standing to the westward with the wind at SSW untill 8 oClock at which time we got Topg^t yards across made all sail and bore away along shore NE for the Easternmost land we had in sight, being at this time in the Latitude of 37° 58' S and Long^{de} of 210° 39' West. The Southernmost Point of land we had in sight which bore from us W ¼ S I judged to lay in the Latitude of 38° 0 Sⁿ and in the Longitude of 211° 07' W. from the Meridion of Greenwich. I have named it Point Hicks because Lieut. Hicks was the first who discover'd this land... To the Southward of this point we could see no land and yet it was very clear in that quarter and by our Longitude compared with that of Tasman the body of Vandiemens Land ought to have bore due south from us and from the soon falling off of the sea after the wind abated I had reason to think it did, but as we did not see it and finding the coast to trend NE and SW or rather more to the Westward makes me doubtfull whether they are one land or no : however every one who compares this Journal with that of Tasmans will be as good a judge I am but it is necessary to observe that I do not take the situation of Vandiemens from the prented charts but from the extract of Tasmens Journal published by Dirk Rembrantse... What we have as yet seen of this land appears rather low and not very hilly, the face of the country green and woody but the sea shore is all white sand.

from the Journal of the First Voyage of Captain James Cook

1 Australia's long coastline offers near endless variety of spectacular views, with sandy beaches alternating with steep rocky cliffs against which the mighty surf pounds with never diminishing force. The scene here illustrates one of these coastal landscapes near Cape Northumberland in southeastern South Australia.

2 The Twelve Apostles are one of the best known and most dramatic coastal scenes of Australia. The twelve rock pillars which once formed part of the landmass have withstood the attack of the waves for the time being, while the coastline is gradually receding.

3 The Flinders Ranges in South Australia are one of the main landscape attractions of this state. The landforms are dominated by steep rugged quartzite ranges, the dark red cliffs of which rise prominently above the much smoother landforms that are formed on soft rocks such as siltstone. The quartzite ranges illustrated here form the eastern fringes of Wilpena Pound, a near circular basin surrounded by steep cliffs on all sides. The low hill in the foreground is known as 'Little Fuji' because of its resemblance to a volcanic cone.

4 Waterfalls are not a common feature of the Australian landscape and are restricted to the eastern uplands where the steep fall to the coast and high rainfall provide the necessary conditions. The Millstream Falls shown here receive their water from the Atherton Tableland and fall in numerous cascades to the coastal foreland.

5 The Willama Falls are amongst the largest waterfalls in Australia. Their free fall is 276 metres and together with some smaller falls they drop by 345 metres.

6 Mt Gambier, the centre of the southeast of South Australia, is picturesquely situated at the margins of a large twin crater. Mt Gambier volcano was active during the Pleistocene and the last activity took place only a few thousand years ago. An interesting but so far unexplained feature of the large crater lake is the dramatic colour change from green in the winter months to deep blue in the summer.

4
5

Geography and Vegetation

The attraction and beauty of the Australian physical environment is quite unlike that of other countries. It lies in the solitude of its harsh and rugged landscape, its endless plains and dunefields and their juxtaposition to white salt lakes or abruptly rising rocky inselbergs, its vast Eucalyptus forests and woodlands and its formidable coastline where mighty cliffs alternate with beautiful beaches. However, distances are vast and the rate of change in the landscape is extremely slow, and one may have to cover hundreds of kilometres to notice any variation in the landscape. Indeed, some overseas travellers may initially find the Australian landscape, Eucalyptus or Acacia woodlands, rather dull and monotonous.

The first white settlers probably felt very much the same, for in vain did they seek the green meadows of a new South Wales or a new England. It took well over a century for the Europeans to give up this search for a park-like English landscape and look at the Australian scenery in its own right, discovering the fascination of the dry, rugged and harsh landscape and the beauty of the Eucalyptus.

Australia is an 'island' continent surrounded on all sides by oceans and far away from other continental land masses. This isolation dates back to the Cretaceous era when the Australian land mass broke away from the disintegrating 'super continent', Gondwanaland and started to drift northward. This former connection of Australia with the other continents of Gondwanaland (Antarctica, India, Africa and South America) and its subsequent long period of isolation are two of the most important factors to consider in our understanding of its physical environment and, in particular, of its distinctive flora and fauna.

The shape of the Australian land mass is relatively simple and compact. The coastline is mostly straight and uncomplicated and generally follows old geological structures. A few exceptions are the large embayments of the Gulf of Carpentaria and the Spencer and St Vincent Gulfs in South Australia. The transition from the usually narrow coastal belt to the dry interior is mostly abrupt and only along the east coast of the continent do we find a larger and wider coastal belt and a more gradual transition to the drylands.

In comparison with other continents, Australia is an 'incomplete' continent, lacking active volcanoes as well as young alpine fold mountains covered by perennial ice and snow. Even during the ice ages Australia did not have any large-scale glaciations and it therefore did not experience the profound changes to its environment that characterize so much of the northern hemisphere continents.

The lack of young fold mountains and active volcanoes is, however, only temporary in geological terms, since the fold mountains and the volcanic island arcs of New Guinea are part of the Australian land mass in the wider sense, and were connected with it repeatedly during the geological past.

The Australian landscape is dominated by vast plains, lowlands and extensive low tablelands, the monotony of which is occasionally interrupted by isolated hills or low mountain ranges which rise abruptly from their surroundings. Only in the east a more or less continuous belt of mountains, highlands and plateaux occurs, extending from Tasmania in the south to Cape York in the north. The highest mountains of Australia, the Snowy Mountains, lie within this upland zone, and its highest peak, Mt Kosciusko, reaches only the modest height of 2228 metres. The Mt Kosciusko area is also the only part of the Australian mainland that was glaciated during the ice ages.

The Main Landscape Regions

The subdivision of a country into natural or physiographic regions is a well established tool of geographical description as it facilitates the comprehension of large spatial units and the recognition of interrelationships. Even though there may usually be agreement on the existence of certain natural regions their definition and delineation is often quite problematic and depends very much on the criteria used and the necessarily subjective judgment of the individual scientist. The following rather coarse subdivisions of Australia into six main regions is based largely on geological and geomorphological grounds.

The East Coast and the Eastern Uplands

An almost uninterrupted belt of uplands extends along the entire length of the eastern margin of the Australian continent from Tasmania to Cape York over a distance of some 3000 kilometres. The width of this highland zone is about 300 kilometres in the south but northward it becomes progressively narrower until it ends as a narrow range of hills at the northern tip of Cape York. The uplands consist of mountain ranges such as the Snowy Mountains, or tablelands such as the Southern or New England tablelands or structural plateaux such as the Blue Mountains. In other areas the uplands are formed of extensive basalt flows covering older landform elements.

The 'Great Dividing Range' is often represented on maps or described in the literature as an extensive uninterrupted chain of mountains, forming the main watershed between the coastal and interior drainage. However, the watershed only locally coincides with the areas of the highest elevations. In many areas, particularly in northern New South Wales and Queensland, it is situated on a large plain and is not easily discernible in the field.

The eastern uplands plunge steeply to a coastal foreland and plain, and the areas with highest relief, i.e. the greatest height differences, are therefore to be found here. The great relief has allowed the streams and rivers to cut deeply into the landscape and impressive gorge country is often associated with this, particularly in areas where resistant rocks such as sandstone are present. This zone of coastal lowlands backed by abruptly rising mountains that cause substantial orographic precipitation, represents Australia's life arteries. Here are to be found the greatest concentrations of people and industries as well as the most intensive land use. Although this coastal zone only occupies a fifth of the Australian land mass, 70 per cent of its population are concentrated here.

The coastal landscape in the east is one of the most attractive and scenically beautiful areas of Australia. In the south the coastal belt is narrow and picturesque and small bays with idyllic sandy beaches alternate with steep rocky cliffs against which the mighty surf of the Pacific Ocean continuously pounds with great force. The coastal zone winds around large river entrances which are favoured sites for settlements. Northward the coastal belt widens and some larger depositional plains are present and form the basis of an intensive agriculture. The beaches here are also longer, particularly around Brisbane where the Gold and Sunshine Coasts attract many thousands of sun and surf hungry visitors. In the tropical north, sandy beaches are largely absent and large areas along the coastline are covered by mangroves. Seaward at some distance from the coast runs the Great Barrier Reef, the most extensive and one of the most spectacular reef formations of the world, which no visitor to this country should fail to see.

The Eastern Alluvial Plains and Lowlands

The western boundary of the eastern uplands is in many areas much less well defined than its eastern limit. In fact, in many instances the transition from the uplands to the neighbouring plains is so gradual that it cannot be detected in the field. Only in the south the Australian Alps rise steeply from the plains and define a sharp boundary between the two landscape regions.

The Murray Darling Basin which forms the southern part of the region represents a huge alluvial plain which is traversed by rivers in endless meanders. The rivers in the southern section of the basin receive sufficient water from the Snowy Mountains to have a permanent flow. The supply of water into the Murray system has been artificially increased by ponding the waters of the Snowy River, which drains to the coast, and pumping it through long tunnels into the Murray River.

The northern tributaries of the Murray, however, reach the river only during wet years. In dry periods they end in a series of lakes which are lined along the river courses like huge beads on a string. The formation of this extensive alluvial plain probably took place when the rivers had considerably higher discharges than today, because the present supply of alluvial sediments is clearly insufficient to build up such a plain.

Northward the Murray Darling Basin merges into an extensive gently undulating erosional plain which structurally is part of the Great Artesian Basin and which drains into the Lake Eyre Basin. Some low laterite tablelands rise prominantly from the plain and give evidence of a former land surface that probably became lateritized and eventually eroded during the Tertiary era. The erosional plain merges northward into the extensive floodplain system which drains into the Gulf of Carpentaria. The entire plain is a maze of braiding channels separated by slightly higher-lying ground, and during floods the whole system is under water so that the few inhabitants of the area are often cut off for weeks.

The Central Deserts

The transition from the eastern lowlands to the central deserts is gradual, and indeed many parts of the eastern lowlands already contain desert features. The important characteristics of the central deserts are the extensive dunefields, the lack of an integrated drainage system, the large gibber (Aboriginal word for stones) plains and the abruptly rising inselbergs, like the famous Ayers Rock. Also typical, though not restricted to the desert areas, are the silcrete and laterite duricrusted tablelands, the prominent and colourful escarpments of which are a welcome contrast to the monotonous plains. These duricrusts are the result of enrichment and subsequent hardening of certain soil horizons with silica and iron during periods of intensive weathering. Silica-rich duricrusts are called silcrete, iron-rich crusts laterite.

Another important feature of the desert zone is the presence of several huge salt lakes or salinas, the largest of which is Lake Eyre. Most impressive features, however, are the seemingly endless dunefields which form an approximate semicircle around the heart of the continent. The dune system is one of the most extensive and most regular in the world and individual dunes often stretch without break over 100 or even 200 kilometres. The trend of the dunes is easterly in the south, turning anticlockwise to the north-east, north and eventually west, and approximately follows the main wind directions initiated by the anticyclones that dominate the weather pattern of central and southern Australia. Presently, little sand movement takes place and the dunes are fixed by vegetation. Only some dune crests show evidence of recent active sand transport. The main periods of sand movement date back to the ice ages and probably coincided with times of greater aridity. The last major period of dune building was between about 18,000 and 16,000 years ago.

The Western Plateau and the Nullarbor Plain

The western plateau rises to an average of 300–500 metres above sea level and constitutes a huge gently undulating erosional plain (peneplain) surrounded occasionally by low quartzitic and granitic hills and ridges. Geomorphologically the plateau consists of two parts: a higher and older plateau, the surface of which is formed by laterite duricrust and a younger plateau which is etched from the older plateau and separated from it by the characteristic 'breakaways' which are similar to the silcrete escarpments west of Lake Eyre.

The so-called river lakes are another typical feature of the plateau. These river lakes are series of long, narrow, often curved salt lakes and clay pans which occupy former drainage lines. The general trend and slope of the river lakes indicate that the former drainage systems must have been linked with land masses to the south and north-west of the present continent and it is therefore assumed that they represent relict river courses dating back to the Mesozoic era when Australia was connected with India and the Antarctic.

Large parts of the western plateau are desert-like, and poor sandy soils cover most areas. The only agriculturally productive country is to be found in the south-west corner, the wheat belt, which receives a reasonably reliable winter rainfall but heavy application of fertilizer is necessary to guarantee a satisfactory harvest.

The Nullarbor Plain is a vast, featureless, largely treeless limestone plain south of the plateau. It is a structural plain which means that the present land surface coincides closely, though it may not be identical with, the original depositional surface of the limestone. Erosion has not modified the plain to any great degree since it rose from the sea, except for some subsurface solution processes that have led to the formation of sinkholes, caves and underground rivers. The Nullarbor Plain ends to the south with a huge cliff which is over 100 metres high and which runs without interruption along the entire length of the Great Australian Bight.

The South Australian Peninsulas and Uplands

This region encompasses the important landscape of South Australia: the Eyre and York Peninsulas and the uplands of the Mt Lofty and Flinders Ranges and their forelands. The Eyre and York Peninsulas represent, geologically, the easternmost extension of the great West Australian Shield and accordingly they are underlain by Archaean rocks. The predominant landforms are undulating plains with quartzitic ranges and granitic inselbergs rising abruptly from them. The inselbergs exhibit interesting and peculiar weathering features like Tafoni (weathering caves), gnammas (weathering hollows) and massive exfoliation plates which seem to peel off the rounded granite hills like the skin of an onion. Most impressive is the occurrence of overhanging rock faces at the base of some inselbergs such as on Pildappa Hill and Uncontitchie Hill. The overhangs, popularly known as wave hills, are caused by relatively rapid weathering at the moist rock-soil interface which receives substantial run-off from the bare rock surface of the inselberg, followed by lowering of the land surface.

Large parts of the Eyre and York Peninsulas and the western foreland of the Mt Lofty Ranges are covered with low sand dunes which do not move at present. They were formed in the Pleistocene era during periods of greater aridity. The indiscriminate clearing of their mallee vegetation and the use of the land for wheat growing has led to a reactivation of the sand movement on the dunes.

The Mt Lofty Ranges are a rolling to low hilly upland with smooth gentle slopes and broad valleys, some of which, like Piccadilly Valley near Adelaide, look very much like a European countryside with their dense pattern of small market gardens. In the southern part of the Mt Loftys the upland plateau character becomes even more obvious, with some larger laterite tablelands. The surface of these tablelands represents the relics of a former more extensive land surface that was uplifted during the Tertiary era and has since been dissected. This surface also continues into Kangaroo Island where it is well preserved because of the low relief.

The Flinders Ranges are higher, more rugged and steeper than their southern counterpart. They are formed of mainly northerly trending high quartzite and sandstone ridges, and intervening lower areas comprising flat to undulating plains or low hills and ridges on relatively soft rocks. The quartzite ridges tend to be asymmetric, with precipitous escarpments on one side and opposing smooth and less steep slopes on the other. The landforms of the Flinders Ranges are structural in origin and there are many beautiful examples of the inter-relationships of structure and landforms to demonstrate this. The structures have been exposed by differential erosion, which means that the processes of weathering and denudation closely followed the underlying rock structures, eroding soft rocks much more rapidly than hard, resistant rocks. In the Flinders Ranges too, there is some evidence of older erosion surfaces predating the uplift, but dating is very difficult.

The Northern Plateaux and Basins

The northern plateaux and basins form a geomorphic and climatic unit quite distinct from the arid and semi-arid plains to the south. The climate here is already tropical, with extensive summer rainfalls. Geomorphologically the region represents a series of plateaux and basins.

23   24

eucalypts and the environmental conditions under which they occur vary greatly. They grow in the tropical and subtropical rain forest, form the upper tree line in the mountains, cover many areas of the semi-arid zone and are also common in the arid areas. They may grow as small, branching shrubs or as tall, stately trees reaching up to 100 metres in height. The Australian eucalypts are popularly known by names such as gum, ash, box, stringybark or ironbark, according to the type and appearance of their bark. Gums are usually trees that have completely shed their bark and therefore often have a brilliant white, smooth trunk, like the well known river red gums that fringe the river courses in the semi-arid and arid zones. The differences between the others depend on both bark texture and the degree to which the bark is shed, thus on stringybarks, the main trunk and larger branches remain covered with dead bark, ironbarks are nearly completely covered with a thick deeply fissured bark, and boxes have thinner, often flaky bark, which either persists to the smaller branches or remains only on the main trunk.

The leaves of the eucalypts mostly hang down more or less vertically and therefore do not provide much shade, a feature which is so alien to the European. This vertical position of the leaves is an adaptation to minimize the leaf surface exposed to the strong rays of the sun and thus prevent excessive water loss by transpiration. Many eucalypt leaves also contain etheric oils and some species known as peppermints are exploited commercially for the extraction of the well known eucalyptus oil. The small round flowers are very characteristic and consist of a bunch of dense filaments – the stamen – yellow, white or red in colour. The fruits vary greatly in form and shape and are important species indicators. Natural hybridization is common, making the task of taxonomists very difficult.

Closely related to the eucalypt is the teatree (Leptospermum), which commonly forms the dense understorey in humid coastal areas. The leaves are said to have been used by Captain Cook for tea making, which has led to its popular name. The paperbarks (Melaleuca), which are most common in the swamp areas of the tropical north, also belong to the same family (Myrtaceae) as do the bottlebrushes (Callistemon) which have become popular plants in suburban gardens.

The genus Acacia is represented by approximately 700 species, more even than Eucalyptus. Acacias are, however, not endemic to Australia but are common in many other parts of the world, particularly in the arid and semi-arid environments of Africa. The acacias also have different popular names such as brigalow, blackwood, mulga and wattle, but these names are not as specific in their usage as the popular names of the eucalypts.

The acacias are characterized by their fragrant, bright yellow flower clusters which consist of numerous small balls of long filaments. The growth forms of the acacias vary as much as those of the eucalypts. Low trees like the mulga *(Acacia aneura)* and crooked, spiky shrubs like *Acacia tetragonophylla* which is popularly known as

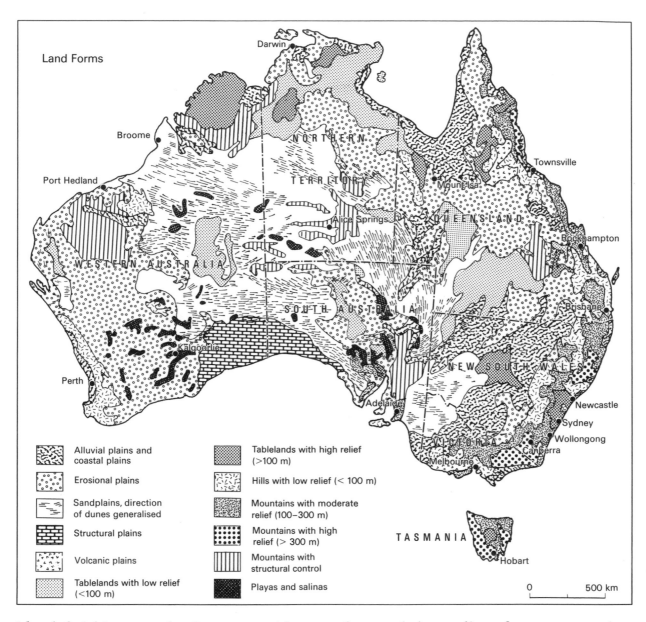

Land Forms

Alluvial plains and coastal plains		Tablelands with high relief (>100 m)	
Erosional plains		Hills with low relief (< 100 m)	
Sandplains, direction of dunes generalised		Mountains with moderate relief (100–300 m)	
Structural plains		Mountains with high relief (> 300 m)	
Volcanic plains		Mountains with structural control	
Tablelands with low relief (<100 m)		Playas and salinas	

0   500 km

'dead finish', occur in the most arid part of central Australia, often representing the only woody plants there. Other acacias like the blackwood wattle *(Acacia melanoxylon)* form large forest trees and their beautiful timber is highly prized and in great demand.

No other woody plants in Australia equal the eucalypts and acacias in numbers or significance. Locally important is the indigenous conifer Callitris, which occurs commonly on the western slopes of the eastern uplands and sporadically throughout the arid zone. Casuarinas, popularly known as oaks, have a superficial resemblance to conifers and occur in a great variety of environments. Best known is the river oak *(Casuarina cunninghamiana)* which is common along the river courses of the eastern uplands and coastal plains.

The Proteaceae, which are represented by the genera Grevillea, Hakea and Banksia, among others, also form woody plants, mostly low shrubs. They too have become popular garden plants. Economically important are the silky oak *(Grevillea robusta)* which occurs in the high rainfall east coast forests, and the Queensland Macadamia, which bears a tasty and increasingly popular nut. The famous Waratah *(Telopea speciosissima)*, whose red, beautiful hemispherical inflorescence forms the floral emblem of New South Wales, also belongs to this family.

The legumes equal the acacias in their multitude of species and their variety in growth forms is even greater. They vary from the well known Sturt's Desert Pea *(Clianthus formosus)*, which is the floral emblem of South Australia, to mighty trees in the tropical rain forest providing excellent timber. Also in the rain forest are some magnificent climbers, among which the species of Millettia is the most attractive and best known.

Compositae represent an important component of the desert vegetation, where their seeds can survive through long periods of drought. After rain they germinate and grow quickly to transform the desert into a sea of flowers. In the mountains too, flowers of this family contribute to the summer beauty of the alpine meadows. Common species are the silver daisy and the cushion plant Erwatia.

The main vegetation types follow closely the main climatic zones. The nomenclature for the different vegetation types is not uniform and depends largely on whether structural or floristic classification criteria are used. The following classification is based on simple structural and in some instances floristic criteria and uses popularly known terms such as mallee and mulga.

Forests, in the sense of dense assemblages of high trees, are almost entirely restricted to the eastern uplands and their steep coastal slopes because it is only here that the high moisture requirements of this vegetation type are met. Large areas of forest have already been cleared, giving way to settlements and intensively used agricultural land. The steeper slopes, however, have so far been largely spared. To the north, tropical and subtropical rain forest flourishes mainly on the east-facing slopes of the coastal ranges. These rain forests typically have a high, dense tree canopy and abundant epiphytes and climbers.

The undergrowth is relatively more open and ferns are common. The density of the undergrowth of the tropical rain forest is often overestimated because along its margins it usually exhibits an impenetrable wall of trees, shrubs and climbers. Inside the forest, however, this density is not achieved because, in contrast to conditions on the forest margin, sunlight penetration here is poor and restricts the development of plant life. The abundance and variety of tree species in tropical rain forests is well known and the Australian rain forest is no exception. It contains a substantial number of Indo-Malayan elements as well as Australian, but no attempt will be made here to list the numerous species.

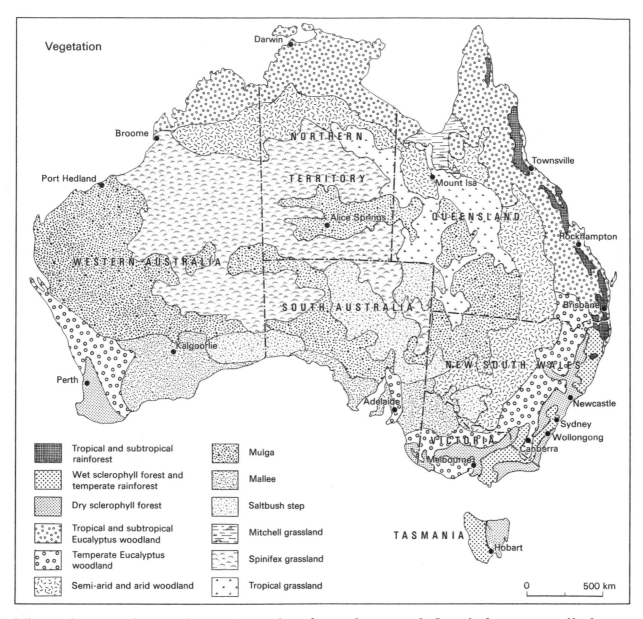

Vegetation

DARWIN
Broome
Port Hedland
NORTHERN
TERRITORY
Townsville
Mount Isa
QUEENSLAND
Alice Springs
Rockhampton
WESTERN AUSTRALIA
SOUTH AUSTRALIA
Brisbane
Kalgoorlie
NEW SOUTH WALES
Perth
Newcastle
Adelaide
Sydney
Wollongong
VICTORIA
Canberra
Melbourne
TASMANIA
Hobart

Tropical and subtropical rainforest
Mulga
Wet sclerophyll forest and temperate rainforest
Mallee
Dry sclerophyll forest
Saltbush step
Tropical and subtropical Eucalyptus woodland
Mitchell grassland
Temperate Eucalyptus woodland
Spinifex grassland
Semi-arid and arid woodland
Tropical grassland

0   500 km

The subtropical rain forest is replaced at about 32° South by a so-called wet sclerophyll forest (wet eucalypt forest) which structurally resembles the rain forest. However, floristically the forest is considerably poorer and is composed of different elements which include not only the dominating eucalypt but also relict elements of an Antarctic flora such as Nothofagus. Mosses and ferns are also common. The eucalypts often reach considerable heights and *Eucalyptus regnans,* commonly known as mountain ash, is one of the tallest trees in the world.

The rain forest and the wet sclerophyll forest merge inland into the dry sclerophyll forest (dry eucalypt forest) and the transition often takes place over a very short distance, reflecting the sudden drop in rainfall as one moves inland. The tree vegetation of the dry sclerophyll forest is again dominated by eucalypts which are considerably lower (usually less than thirty metres) and more widely spaced than in the vegetation types to the east. The ground cover already is distinctly xeromorphic and regular burning is a characteristic feature. Like other drier vegetation types the dry sclerophyll forest shows a remarkable resistance and tolerance to fire and some species in it only germinate after fire.

The dry sclerophyll forest is replaced further inland by a vegetation type known in Australia as woodlands. These are open 'forests' with low, often widely spaced, trees and undergrowth of grass and/or low shrubs. The term 'savanna' has also been used but it signifies a more open vegetation type such as the African savanna. According to the climatic environment, one can distinguish between tropical and subtropical woodlands, temperate woodlands and semi-arid and arid woodlands. Most woodlands are dominated by eucalypts and acacias, but other genera such as Casuarina, Melaleuca, Heterodendrum and Callitris may also dominate.

Similar to, and often transitional with, the woodlands are the shrublands. They are also composed of woody plants which are relatively low (two to eight metres) and which usually do not have a main trunk but branch out from the base into numerous small stems. The two main types are the mallee and the mulga, both of which are typical Australian vegetation types, hence the adoption of the Aboriginal terms. The mallee is a dense eucalypt shrubland which sometimes has the appearance of a forest, especially when the shrubs are relatively high. The mallee was very extensive on the Murray plains and much of the area is popularly still referred to as mallee; but land clearance has drastically reduced its area. Dominant species include *Eucalyptus socialis, E. oleosa, E. dumosa* and *E. diversifolia.*

The mulga is a more open vegetation type, similar to open woodlands, and is dominated by acacias, among which *Acacia aneura* and *Acacia brachystachya* are the most common. *A. aneura* is so dominant that it is popularly referred to as mulga. A third type of shrubland is the shrub steppe which consists of low shrubs of saltbush *(Atriplex vesicaria)* and bluebush (*Maireana* [formerly *Kochia*] spp.). Like the mallee, it is a shrubland because the dominant species are woody and multistemmed. They never exceed two metres in height, so it is called a low shrubland. The arid centre is dominated by grassland. Scattered trees and shrubs of eucalypt and, particularly, acacia, are nearly always present and the Australian desert landscape therefore never looks as desolate and bare as do deserts in other parts of the world. The two main grassland types are the Mitchell Grasslands (Astrebla) which occupy the subtropical north-east and the Spinifex Grassland (Triodia) which covers the endless dunefields and sand plain of the centre.

Besides these common vegetation types which cover vast areas, there are a few which are of local occurrence and tied to particular environments and local climatic conditions, such as the mangrove vegetation in the tidal zone or the alpine heath and tundra vegetation on the high mountains.

The mangroves are largely restricted to the tropical and subtropical zones where they form a narrow belt of trees and shrubs in the tidal zone. Mangrove species are true cosmopolitans and occur all over the world under similar environmental conditions. Most mangroves show a distinct zonation in their species composition from the open water inland. The pioneer genera are Avicennia and Sonneratia which form the outer margins of the mangrove and extend furthest seaward. They are followed landward by Rhizophora and Brugiera forming the core of the mangroves. The mangrove swamps often merge further landwards into brackish and eventually freshwater swamps, in which trees like milkwood (Excoecaria), Melaleuca and Casuarina dominate.

The alpine heaths and tundras occupy only very small areas of the Australian continent, being restricted to altitudes above 1400–1500 metres on the mainland and about 1100 metres in Tasmania. Low shrubs, herbs and cushion plants are the main constituents of this vegetation type, which in summer forms a magnificent carpet of flowers.

---

28 The Black Swan is unique to Australia, although it is now a common sight in zoos and parks around the world. It is still most numerous in its original habitat, the Swan River of Western Australia, and features in the emblem of this State.

29 A common Australian water bird is the egret, which occurs frequently in the north of the continent. Shown here is one of the most common species, the little egret *(Egretta garzetta)*.

30 Parrots and lorikeets are common all over the Australian continent and often move in noisy flocks of hundreds of birds. The rainbow-lori *(Trichoglossus haematodus)* is a particularly colourful example.

31 Australia has a rich dragon fauna with about 40 different species. Although some dragons can grow to 90 cm in length most are short and do not exceed 15 cm when fully grown, like this dragon lizard *(Amphibolurus barbatus)*.

32 The crocodile is at home in the tropical north of Australia where it inhabits the tidal waters and estuaries. Only the large saltwater crocodile shown here is dangerous to man.

33 The grotesque thorny devil *(Moloch horridus)*, another dragon, is a tiny harmless lizard living on termites.

34 One of the best known Australian animals and one that enjoys world-wide affection is the koala seen here relaxing in tree forks high up above the ground. Because of indiscriminate hunting the koala was close to extinction but is now totally protected and has recovered remarkably well.

35 The kangaroo undoubtedly is the best known Australian animal and is also the most common of the large animals. Ecologically it occupies a similar position to the large herbivores of the northern continents.

36 The coral islands of the Great Barrier Reef are the breeding grounds for several species of marine turtle. A green turtle is shown here laying its eggs in the soft coral sand of the popular holiday resort Heron Island.

37 The tiger cat *(Dasyurus viverrinus)* is one of the few surviving carnivorous marsupials living in the forest areas of Tasmania and along the southeast coast of the mainland. It is a nocturnal, very shy animal sheltering during the day in hollow logs or under rocks. Its brown fur is dotted with white spots, hence its name.

38 The lyrebird *(Menura novaehollandiae)* lives in the dense forest of the east coast and is well known for its superb display of plumage (only the male) during courting time. The lyrebird is also a master of mimicry and it is said that it can even imitate human voices.

39 The platypus *(Ornithorhynchus anatinus)* is one of only two existing egg-laying mammals (monotremes). It is now quite common in many inland waters after having been close to extinction due to indiscriminate hunting for its soft fur.

40 The echidna or spiny ant eater *(Tachyglossus aculeatus)* is also a monotreme like the platypus. In spite of its resemblance to the placental hedgehog there is no relation between the two animals. The echidna and the hedgehog are good examples of the phenomena known as convergent evolution.

28

29

30

31

32

33

34

35

36

37

The Australian Fauna

The Australian fauna is unique and reflects, like the vegetation, the long isolation of the continent and its development and evolution without interference from outside. The present fauna originates from two main sources, the Gondwanaland continent on the one hand and the Asiatic continent on the other. The relationship between the Australian fauna of Southern Africa and South America is well demonstrated in a number of animals, most notably the flightless birds like the ostriches of South Africa, the rheas in South America and emus and cassowaries in Australia and New Guinea, as well as the kiwis and the extinct moas of New Zealand. The Asiatic source was periodically connected with Australia via a land bridge over the Indo-Malayan Archipelago which broke up in the late Tertiary era. Since then, some 'island-hopping' migration has continued but has had little overall effect on the composition of the Australian fauna.

Origins

The relative isolation that followed the destruction of the 'land-bridge' allowed evolution to continue without serious competition from other animals such as the placental eutherians (or 'true' mammals) which grew to dominate the major part of the rest of the world. Most importantly the larger Australian animals were allowed to evolve in the absence of carnivores. The Tasmanian wolf (Thylacine), the largest marsupial carnivore, now on the verge of extinction in its last refuge in south-west Tasmania, is not thought to have been a serious predator of the large kangaroos or emus, though its importance is by no means clear.

A comparison between the fauna of Australia, particularly the vertebrate fauna, and that of Europe and North America and North Africa, reveals an interesting phenomenon known as convergent evolution. This means that under similar environmental conditions animals of completely different families may develop a similar behaviour or even a similar outward appearance. Niches similar to those occupied by the large grazing ungulates of the northern hemisphere were occupied in Australia by kangaroos. The hedgehog of Europe is in outward appearance very like the echidna, but the echidna is one of only two egg-laying mammals in existence (the platypus is the other). Even more striking is the similarity in outward appearance and ecological behaviour between the placental and marsupial moles. Not only ecological and anatomical adaptations have paralleled those of the eutherians, but behavioural and physiological features as well. It is this remarkable convergent evolution which has recently led scientists to conclude that, far from representing a primitive, or serial stage, in the evolution of 'true' mammals, marsupials are a well advanced group in their own right and have been genetically separate from some common parent stock for more than 100 million years.

The Amphibians

The only native amphibians in Australia are the frogs. So far, 131 species in twenty-two genera have been described, but as investigation progresses the number is bound to increase. Although most frogs are found in areas with relatively high, regular rainfall, some have managed to adapt to the arid desert environments of the continent and many avoid desiccation by burrowing. One species, *Cyclorana platycephales* fills its bladder and the space between its intestines and body wall with water. Within its burrow it wraps itself in a cocoon to reduce further water loss; a most astonishing adaptation to the arid environment.

The Reptiles

Australia has a rich reptile fauna which is a mixture of very ancient forms that have been on the continent a long time, and more recent migrants from the islands to the north. Altogether there are 395 species in ninety-five genera. There are two crocodiles. The saltwater crocodile is common throughout Asia, and occurs on the coast and in the estuarine waters across northern Australia. These can be a danger to man. The freshwater crocodile, on the other hand, is harmless. It occupies freshwater streams, lagoons and billabongs, mostly on the eastern and southern shores of the Gulf of Carpentaria.

Apart from thirteen tortoises and one turtle found in streams, swamps and ponds, Australian seas are inhabited by all five species of marine turtle, and the sole species of leathery turtle. The leathery turtle is the largest living turtle, occasionally exceeding 680 kilograms in weight and 224 centimetres in length. Although it is common in Australian seas, it is not thought to breed there.

Australian lizards can be divided into five families: geckos, snake-lizards, dragons, goannas and skinks. The geckos are a cosmopolitan family of about 650 species, at least fifty of which are found in Australia. They are small, nocturnal, non-venomous lizards which feed mostly on insects. They are often brightly coloured and some have almost transparent skin.

The thirteen species of snake-lizards are restricted to Australia and New Guinea. They are small lizards (less than 75 centimetres long) with rudimentary hind-limbs and no sign at all of forelimbs. Thus, they closely resemble small snakes. Generally, they are nocturnal and insectivorous. Australia, with forty species, has the richest dragon fauna in the world. They are active, diurnal lizards, some growing to over 90 centimetres and some as small as 12 centimetres. Many are brightly coloured with spines on the body and some have spectacular neck ruffs. The mountain devil is an exceptionally colourful and grotesque desert specimen.

The largest goanna in the world is the Indonesian Komodo dragon, which can reach over 300 centimetres in length. The Australian Perentie, however, is not far behind, having been measured at nearly 250 centimetres. The smallest measures only 20 centimetres when fully grown. Goannas fulfil a scavenger role but do feed on living prey as well. There are 150 species of skink in Australia and they occur in numerous different shapes, colours and sizes. Many are small with short legs and shiny scales. Others, such as the blue-tongued lizard and the stumpy lizard, are heavily built but with a clumsy appearance, though they can move quickly for short distances.

The Australian snakes are well known and much feared because they are amongst the most poisonous snakes in the world. Elapid snakes of the family Elapidae are characterized by a pair of hollow or grooved fangs connected to poison glands. The family includes well known African and Asian snakes such as cobras, but the venom of both the Australian tiger snake and the Australian taipan are more potent than these. There are eight other species known to have killed humans in Australia; some, such as the eastern brown snake, the black snake and the copperhead are relatively common. Sea-snakes, found in the north coastal waters, in estuaries and sometimes on land, are also venomous. There are approximately twenty species occurring in the Indo-Pacific region, any of which may be found in Australian waters. There are two other families of snakes in Australia, the pythons and the tree snakes and water snakes. Some members of the latter have potent venom, but it is not thought to be lethal to man. The pythons are non-venomous snakes which kill their prey by squeezing it to death. They eat birds, mammals and other reptiles. The rock python of Queensland can grow to over 750 centimetres whilst the Pigmy Python seldom exceeds 60 centimetres.

The Birds

The Australian birds are famous for their beautiful, brightly coloured plumage and their wonderful songs. They are, therefore, in high demand as pets in Australia and overseas. There is no list which is sure to include every Australian bird species, though a working list prepared in 1969 by CSIRO recognizes 708 species in seventy-nine families. A number of these families are endemic to Australia, or Australia and New Guinea. It is these birds, along with a number of members of other more cosmopolitan families, which characterize the Australian avifauna.

Not all Australian birds are bright and colourful, and the large flightless birds are certainly one example. The emus, the largest living birds after the African ostriches, live in open woodland and scrubland. The male emu incubates the eggs and may go without food for up to eight weeks while fulfilling this duty. Although they have disappeared from the more closely settled parts of Australia, and from Tasmania, they are still numerous in some districts, numerous enough in Western Australia to be a serious pest to wheat growers in some years. The cassowary found in Australia is called the double-wattled cassowary. It too is a flightless bird, though not as big as the emu. It occurs in dense rainforest and, though common in some restricted areas, is shy and seldom seen.

Australia is relatively poor in waterfowl, supporting only nineteen species, but of these five are endemic and one other occurs outside the continent only in southern New Guinea. This latter, the magpie goose, is a unique bird, occupying a sub-family all of its own. Scientists consider that, although evolved from the ancestors common to other waterfowl, it branched off before true geese and ducks were differentiated.

Most interesting ecologically are the mound-builders. These birds are characterized by their practice of incubating eggs with natural heat produced in mounds they construct for the purpose. There are three species in Australia, the scrub fowl which range throughout Indo-Malaya and parts of Polynesia, the brush turkey, a rain forest bird, and the mallee fowl. The mallee fowl has declined greatly in numbers due to the clearing of its mallee and mallee-scrub habitat for grazing and cropping.

A European visiting Australia for the first time cannot help but be impressed with the numerous noisy, brightly coloured lorikeets, cockatoos and parrots. Lorikeets feed mainly on pollen and nectar, utilizing their specialized 'brush' tongue, though they do also eat fruit. They are arboreal and gregarious, moving swiftly and often noisily in large flocks to wherever there is pollen or nectar.

Cockatoos are much larger birds. Some are arboreal and some feed mainly on the ground. They are all highly gregarious, though the arboreal species such as the palm cockatoo and the gang-gang occur in smaller groups than the ground feeding species. These latter may be seen in flocks of thousands, making deafening noises. The distinctive galahs with their bright pink chest, grey back and white head and crest can sometimes be serious grain pests, capable of decimating a wheat crop. The cockatoo is a very popular pet because of its ability to imitate the human voice. Parrots are a more diverse group than the others. Some, such as the budgerigar, are just as gregarious as galahs, while others, like the crimson rosella, a deep red and bright blue bird of the forests, are more often seen in pairs or small groups of four or five.

One of the most remarkable birds in Australia is the lyrebird. There are two species: the superb lyrebird, which occurs in forests along the east coast from southern Queensland to Melbourne, and the Albert lyrebird, which has a restricted occurrence in the rain forest around the Queensland-New South Wales border. Apart from their magnificent lyre tail (which only the male has) these birds are famous for their mimicry. They mimic the songs of many other forest birds, and according to popular folk-lore can mimic the voices of men.

Another characteristic Australian bird family is that of the honeyeaters. They have a long brush tongue and all feed, at least sometimes, on nectar and pollen though many, particularly the larger species, mainly eat insects and/or fruit. Various Australian plants are especially adapted for pollination by birds, particularly honeyeaters, many of which are closely associated with particular plant communities in particular seasons.

The bower-birds are unique to Australia and New Guinea. They are forest birds, often occurring only in dense rain forest. The satin bower-bird, though, is reasonably common in the coastal regions of New South Wales and Victoria. This bird constructs a 'stage' of sticks between or at one end of an avenue of parallel walls, also constructed of sticks. It then stocks this 'bower' with shiny, usually blue, objects (e.g. shells, scraps of paper and plastic). The bower is used as a display stage in courtship proceedings.

The Australian coastline is a breeding ground or resting place for a great variety of sea birds. Altogether there are 104 species. These include rare penguin visitors from Antarctic waters (only the little penguin is known to breed on the Australian coast), the wandering albatross, whose wingspan reaches 230 centimetres, and the majestic Australian pelican whose soaring flights may reach 3000 metres.

The Mammals

Australia is the only continent where representatives of all three kinds of mammal are to be found: monotremes, marsupials and placentals or eutherians. Australia's isolation has produced a fauna very different from that of the rest of the world. It is dominated by marsupials; there are two monotremes, and a number of eutherians – mainly bats, rats and introduced, mainly European, pests.

The monotremes are mammals which lay eggs yet still suckle their young. There are only two monotremes in existence, the echidna and the platypus, and their ancestry is remarkably obscure since there is no fossil evidence to trace their origins. Echidnas are also called spiny ant-eaters and porcupines. They have spines covering their backs though the under-surface is covered in coarse hair. They feed mainly on ants, which they collect on a long extensile tongue. They average about forty-five centimetres in length and weigh about 6.3 kilograms. The platypus lives in lakes and streams in eastern Australia. It too is small, measuring only about fifty-five to sixty-five centimetres when fully grown. The platypus feeds on insect larvae, crustacea, worms, etc., which it finds by muzzling the mud and gravel of creeks and ponds with its duck-bill, a highly touch-sensitive organ made of thick, flexible, naked skin. It was once hunted for its fur, but since it has been totally protected by law its numbers have increased, so that now it is quite common over most of its range though still hard to see due to its shy habits. The male platypus has a poisonous spine on the inside of its hind legs which can cause a painful wound. This is only used when the animal feels threatened.

Marsupials display a pattern of evolution and organization quite distinct from that of other mammals, yet their adaptations to particular environments closely resemble those of other mammals. Australian marsupials range from large nomadic grazers, such as the red kangaroo, to the remarkable desert-dwelling marsupial mole. The best known and most common marsupials are the kangaroos and wallabies. They are a large and diverse group thought to have evolved from ancestors common to the possums. The different kangaroos and wallabies are mainly distinguished according to size and colour.

There are five kangaroos: the eastern and western greys of savanna woodlands and eucalypt forests; the euro or wallaroo, found in rocky gullies and bare tablelands and hill country; the red kangaroo of arid and semi-arid open woodlands, open shrublands and grasslands; and the antelope kangaroo of the northern savannas and grasslands.

One of the most fascinating adaptations of the kangaroos to the difficult environment is a phenomenon known as delayed implantation or embryonic diapause. This permits the female to delay the development of the embryo after conception, so preventing her having to carry and feed two young at the same time. It also permits survival, in exceptionally difficult drought years, without the additional strain imposed by young.

The smaller wallabies, which encompass eight species, mostly live in the denser forest and bush of the coastal zones and eastern uplands. Even more closely associated with the forest environment are the tree kangaroos, which have long front legs and a long prehensile tail which is used as a support while climbing. The smallest members of the kangaroo family are the rat kangaroos, which are often only thirty centimetres long. They live on insects and larvae and are well adapted to survival in an arid environment. They stay in small burrows during daytime to minimize water loss and come out to feed in the late evening and early morning.

The large kangaroos have probably suffered least from European man in Australia. They have even benefited by the creation of pastures and watering holes, so that despite the well-publicized slaughter of great numbers a few years ago, grey kangaroos and possibly red kangaroos are thought to be more common now than they were at the time of white man's settlement.

Many other marsupials, however, have not fared so well. The clearing of forests and woodland; the cultivation of grain crops; and competition and predation from introduced animals such as the rabbit, the cat, the fox and the dog, have caused a sharp decline in many populations of smaller marsupials. Marsupial mice and native cats (not true cats at all) have suffered greatly. The native cats have suffered most from destruction of habitat, but also from competition from domestic cats. They are extremely strong and aggressive predators but are not as adaptable as true cats and have found their sources of food (birds, reptiles and smaller mammals) badly depleted.

The tiny marsupials of the desert have suffered badly with the introduction of domestic grazing animals such as sheep and cattle, the rabbit plagues, and competition from the house mice accompanying settlement. But most still survive in some areas and with the growing concern for wildlife conservation their futures are rosier now than a few years ago. The arboreal marsupials are a diverse group. All marsupials are thought to have originally descended from arboreal ancestors. The brush-tailed possum is a familiar animal to many Australians who live in suburbs. It has adapted remarkably well, thriving on introduced fruit and blossoms, and taking up residence in roofs. These possums often become very tame, accepting food from the hand (such as bread and honey) and, in this way, make delightful 'wild' pets.

Another type of possum is the glider, so named because it has a membrane of skin which is attached to the outer side of the hand and the ankle. The animal can stretch the membrane by extending arms and legs, and so glide from tree to tree. The smallest glider is the pygmy glider, merely the size of a mouse. The largest is the greater glider, the size of a large cat. It is a remarkably good glider; using its long bushy tail as a rudder it may cover distances of up to 100 metres from tree top to the base of another tree. Naturally enough, gliders and possums are found only in the forested parts of the continent.

A most remarkable example of convergent evolution is the marsupial mole, a small animal only about fifteen centimetres long but with all the anatomical features of true, northern hemisphere moles. Little is known about its habits, physiology or ecology. The few specimens that have been captured have all been found in sand dunes in desert sandhill country.

The koala is probably the most popular Australian animal and, apart from the kangaroo, the best known overseas. Its habitat is the forested area of the eastern uplands, where it lives high above the ground in the tree tops, sitting leisurely in branches. Its food consists entirely of leaves of certain species of eucalypts with a high oil content. The leaves seem to provide the animal with sufficient moisture, for koalas rarely drink water. The koala is a skilled climber but on the ground it is helpless and clumsy. Because of its soft fur, it used to be hunted and it was close to extinction. The total protection it now enjoys has, however, led to a steady increase in its numbers and its survival seems to be assured.

Australia has a number of true 'eutherian' mammals, such as rats and bats. Bats are the only mammals that fly, and there are a wide variety in Australia. The most spectacular are the large flying foxes, some of which have wingspans of more than 120 centimetres, and can be seen in great numbers, in some parts of the continent, in the evening sky. They generally eat blossoms but can be serious pests to fruit-growers by invading orchards of ripening fruit.

41 This aerial view shows the typical zonation of a barrier reef with an outer wind and wave exposed radial zone (left), its sharp boundary to the deep ocean and the inner more irregular reef flat which slopes down gradually into the lagoon. A low island entirely formed of coral debris, a so-called sandy cay, has developed in the extreme southwest (right) of the island. Note that south is to the top of the picture.

42 Underwater view of floating star fishes against the background of corals.

43 Giant clam *(Tridacna gigas)*, one of the largest bivalve shells, with its colourful 'mouth'. The colour is caused by tiny one cellular plants that live in the flesh of the clam. Contrary to popular belief clams are not dangerous to man.

44 During low tide parts of the outer reef area fall dry and one can observe the great variety of corals and other life forms. This picture is from the outer Barrier Reef east of Townsville and illustrates several kinds of staghorn coral.

45 Diving is undoubtedly the most exciting way to explore the wonders of the Barrier Reef. The coral fish are surprisingly little concerned about human invaders and may even be fed by hand.

46 Soldier crabs *(Mictyris longicarpus)* walk along the mud flats in rows that remind one of marching soldiers.

47 Close-up of coral colony of a staghorn coral. The individual coral polyps sit in the tiny cup-shaped depressions that totally surround the coral branches.

48 Corrugations formed by waves and wind along the gently sloping beach.

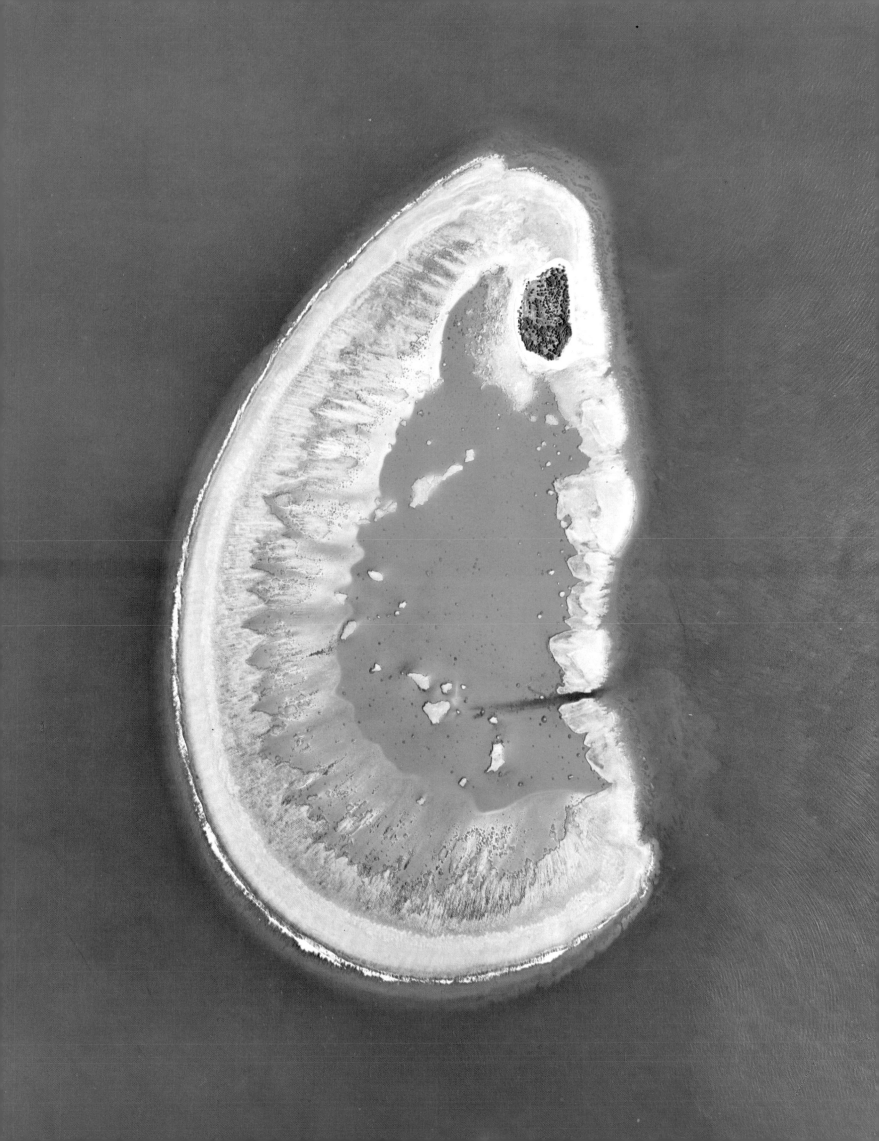

42

43

44

45

46

47 48

The Great Barrier Reef

Australia's Great Barrier Reef is one of the most fascinating and impressive natural features of the world. Indeed, Australians like to proclaim it the eighth wonder of the world. It is difficult to do justice in a verbal account to the beauty of the reefs and the creatures which build and inhabit them. Visitors are invariably thrilled at the exotic splendour of the coral formations and the adjacent islands with their palms and golden beaches.

A walk across a reef at low tide reveals a multitude of sea-dwelling animals, some trapped in pools left by the receding tide, some stuck fast to the coral, waiting for their food to come to them, and others more mysterious, withdrawing behind the coral at the approach of a shadow. When the sea returns, and more water covers the reef, the adventurous visitor can float with a snorkel and mask to discover a seemingly endless array of brightly coloured fish, darting among the coral, beautiful to watch but deadly earnest in their everyday struggle to stay alive.

The reef is not without its perils for humans too. Apart from the swift, voracious sharks, there are many poisonous animals. Some are deceptively beautiful, such as the butterfly cod and stinging sea anemones. The stone fish, appropriately named for its resemblance to a barnacle-encrusted stone, can inject a deadly venom through a spine on its back, and the almost transparent sea wasp, a jellyfish, has been responsible for a number of fatalities in recent years. The dangers should not be overstated, though visitors are well advised always to use footwear and avoid touching or picking up creatures they do not know. In fact there is no need to touch or handle to appreciate the splendour of the reef. Shells and coral do not belong on the mantlepiece.

From an aircraft the Great Barrier Reef can be seen as a series of linear, roundish and oval patches, the light green colour of which contrasts sharply with the surrounding dark blue of the deeper ocean. The eastern margin of the reefs facing the open ocean mostly forms a straight line and is accentuated by the white surf that breaks continuously over it. The landward side is more irregularly shaped and often broken by narrow channels through which the surf rushes with great velocity. The bird's eye view also shows clearly that the Great Barrier Reef is not a continuous barrier but a maze of innumerable individual reefs which rarely form a straight line but are irregularly scattered through the lagoon. Scientists therefore often call this reef system the Great Barrier Reefs or Great Barrier Reeferies in preference to the commonly used singular Great Barrier Reef.

The extent of the Great Barrier Reef is truly gigantic. It stretches from the 22 °S parallel to the south coast of New Guinea over a distance of some 2000 kilometres. The reefs cover an area of over 200,000 square kilometres. In its basic structure the Great Barrier Reef is similar to other smaller barrier reef systems. It runs at some distance from the mainland, more or less parallel to it, and its foundations lie on the continental shelf. The outward, i.e. ocean side, of the reef falls steeply and abruptly to the deep ocean, but landward it dips only gently into the so-called lagoon, which rarely exceeds 100 metres in depth. This lagoon, in Australia also called the Barrier Reef Channel, varies in width from over 100 kilometres in the south to some 40 kilometres further north and eventually narrows north of Cairns. It is therefore not surprising that Captain James Cook, during his epic discovery of the Australian east coast, was completely unaware that he had entered a barrier reef complex until he had sailed hundreds of kilometres northward.

Scattered over the lagoon are numerous other largely roundish reefs and reef patches which sometimes have low, small, coral islands associated with them. These coral islands consist entirely of coral debris: sand, boulders and beach rock which is a cemented coral sand of considerable hardness. These so-called 'low islands' or coral cays are never more than a few hundred metres in diameter, and often as small as a few tenths of metres, and are either devoid of vegetation or are covered by peculiar vegetation types such as the well known Pisonia forest on Heron Island. The coral islands which are in closer proximity to the mainland have, because of easier seed dispersal, a richer vegetation cover like the splendid rain forest on Green Island near Cairns. The great majority of coral cays are uninhabited, but a few are occupied and mostly serve tourism. Some, such as Heron Island, also serve as base for scientific work on the reef.

Approaching the mainland, a different type of island appears, rising prominently from the sea. These are the so-called 'high islands' which are formed of solid rock and which geologically are part of the mainland, but became separated from it because of subsidence of the continental shelf and the postglacial sea level rise. These high islands are surrounded by narrow fringing reefs which also have attractive coral formations and a rich fish life, but not on the grandiose scale to be found on the outer reefs. The mainland is only locally fringed by reefs which are usually poorly developed. The lack of good reef development along the mainland shores is due to the runoff and sedimentation associated with the steeply sloping hinterland.

The structure of the Great Barrier Reef cannot be described without making a brief mention of some general facts on coral reef development. Corals are primitive animals, rarely exceeding one centimetre in diameter, which continually secrete calcium carbonate during their life. Since the coral animals live in fixed positions the secreted carbonate which hardens to limestone accumulates and the total amount of limestone produced by millions and millions of coral animals over thousands of years is therefore very impressive. The main conditions for coral growth are continuously high water temperatures (above 18 °C), and clear and shallow water not exceeding fifty metres in depth, guaranteeing good light penetration. The fact that corals can only live in shallow water originally provided some difficulties in the explanation of thick coral deposits which often exceeded several hundred metres. In recent times thicknesses of coral over 1000 metres have been proven in some atolls of the Pacific. In the Great Barrier Reef thicknesses usually do not exceed 200 metres although 400-metre ones have been found. Among the many theories brought forward in the last century, Darwin's concept has remained the most accepted and is still regarded as essentially correct. He postulated that barrier reefs and atolls are simply former fringing reefs that gradually became separated from the mainland, or in the case of an atoll, from an island, when the land and surrounding sea floor slowly subsided. The vertical reef growth, however, kept pace with the subsidence. In this fashion hundreds and hundreds of metres of coral can be accumulated as long as the subsidence is slow enough not to outpace coral growth. The American, Daly, considered that the essential factor in vertical reef growth is not so much subsidence but the worldwide postglacial rise in sea level caused by the melting of the enormous continental glaciers of the northern hemisphere. Since this rise in sea level only amounts to some 130 metres it cannot fully explain the great thickness of many reefs. However, sea level changes are certainly an additional factor.

Let us turn back to the basic element of reef development – the coral. Corals are bisexual animals and reproduce sexually through sperm and eggs and asexually through budding. The fertilized eggs develop into tiny individuals that float in the water until they find a place to attach themselves; failing this they will die. Once they have settled they immediately start multiplying by budding, and in time a colony of thousands and thousands of individual coral animals, or polyps, will develop, each of which secretes limestone to form the well known coral skeletons. The secretion of lime takes place at the outside, predominantly at the base of the polyps and therefore the entire coral skeleton continually grows outward. Depending on the coral species, the growth per individual animal per year amounts to between one and ten centimetres. Another important, though less obvious, contribution to coral reef development are the coral algae. They live in a kind of symbiosis with the coral, but the exact nature of this is not well known. In many cases the coral algae are responsible for the beautiful colour of the coral, a fact which many disappointed reef fossickers experience when the colourful piece of coral they take home fades on the mantlepiece.

Growth forms of corals vary greatly and it is useless listing the different species without having them illustrated by colour photographs. Even within one species the forms may vary considerably and this represents an additional difficulty for the identification, which we should leave to the specialist. The following is therefore restricted to a few commonly occuring and easily identifiable genera. The most common corals belong to the genus Acropora, which is popularly known as staghorn coral. As the name implies this coral forms upwards-branching staghorn-like structures. Since the individual coral colonies mostly grow close to one another, these staghorns tend to develop into an impenetrable jungle of branches. Some species of Acropora, however, do not branch out as lavishly but develop only short vertical spikes which extend from a main 'stem' that grows in a more or less horizontal position.

Another coral that is easy to recognize is the massive round brain coral which measures about one metre in diameter and half a metre in height. The tiny polyps are situated in curved rows on the outside of the coral block and give it the appearance of a brain. Also massive blocks but more rounded and resembling a huge arctic cushion plant are the Gonipora corals which belong to the few corals that extend their polyps in bright sunlight and can therefore be easily seen on the reef. The mushroom corals (Fungia) are another distinctive genus. They are considerably smaller than most corals, only about five centimetres in diameter, and their skeleton is produced by a single polyp. Their very delicate skeleton resembles the lower side of a mushroom.

Completely different from these lime secreting corals are the soft corals. These are plant-like organisms with thick spongy lobate 'leaves' and they may reach about one metre in height. At low tide when they are exposed to the atmosphere they look rather ugly, but once they are fully submerged and extend their polyps they immediately change into a beautiful and colourful structure.

Similar to the soft corals are the sea anemones, which resemble an anemone flower when their tentacles are extended. The best known species is the large anemone (*Stochactis kenti*) the colour of which may vary from blue to green. The tentacles of the anemone which serve like the tentacles of the corals as food traps and food catchers are poisonous and are therefore quite effective in supplying the colony with small creatures that happen to swim or float past. Surprisingly there are two species of small coral fish that live happily amid the poisonous tentacles without being harmed. The reason for this is not known.

Although the corals are the main building stones of the reefs they are not the only attractions. In fact the fascination of the reef for the visitor may lie to a greater extent in the variety of life forms directly associated with the reef. There are shells, sea stars, trepang, sea urchins, crabs and of course the multitude of fish. The most impressive shells are without doubt the bivalve clamshells, the fragments of which can be found in great concentrations on the shores of coral cays. The living clams are mostly attached to old corals or other coral boulders into which they have bored holes. They stand in an upright position with their 'mouth' opening towards the sky. This opening often exhibits the most beautiful assemblage of colours with predominantly green and blue tones, caused by a great amount of tiny single-cell plants that live in the flesh of the clam. The widespread fear that these clams can be dangerous to man and close like a trap when he steps into the open mouth is not substantiated by fact.

The considerably smaller cone shells which are among the most sought after pieces of the shell collector are, however, not as harmless. Their sharp poisonous spike can inflict painful injuries often associated with partial paralysis and they should be treated with great caution. The cone shells are elegant in their well proportioned cone-like shapes and exhibit beautiful colours and patterns on their shiny outside shell. They are among the most attractive creatures of the reef. Unfortunately, the eagerness of shell collectors and, more recently, the shell collection for commercial exploitation greatly depleted the cone shell population and some of the more highly priced rare species are in serious danger of extinction. The smaller cowrie shell, with its smooth, shiny surface, is a rather common genus and it occupied an important position in the native culture of the Pacific before the advent of the European. Not only was it used for decoration, but also as a type of 'cash' in the native trade.

Oysters cannot compete with the shells mentioned above in respect to beauty, but their tasty flesh is more than compensation for this, especially when eaten fresh on the spot. Similar in appearance are the pearl oysters, although they are not the same species as the edible oysters. Pearl oysters commonly occur in the northern part of the Great Barrier Reef and are collected for commercial purposes by the Torres Strait Islanders. Other interesting shells are the pinkish spider shells, with their thin pointed spikes extending from the shell body, or the fantastically coloured bright red magic carpet or Spanish dancer, or the little horn shells with their spiral growth, and the well known bailer shells which were used by the indigenous people as water bailers. The list of species is nearly inexhaustible, since shells belong to one of the largest classes in the animal world.

Not particularly attractive, even ugly, are the sausage- or cucumber-like trepang (trepang being the Malayan name, it is also known by its French trade-name of *bêche-de-mer*) which lie motionless on the shallow sandy floors of the lagoons. These strange animals measure about thirty to forty centimetres in length and six to eight centimetres in thickness, and like worms they continually swallow sand and mud, from which they withdraw the organic substances as they pass through the body. If they are disturbed, they can throw up their entire 'stomach' contents, including their inner organs, as a defence mechanism, and thus disappear in a cloud of sand. Afterwards the inner organs simply grow again. It is surprising that this unattractive animal with its even less appealing habits is a much sought after delicacy in some Asiatic countries, particularly China, where the dried-out skin is used for a soup. Collection of trepang used to be an important commercial enterprise for the Macassar traders from the Indonesian archipelago, who ventured as far as the north coast of Australia; this led to sporadic, sometimes regular, contact with the Aborigines in pre-European times. The last trepang fleet left Australian waters in 1907.

The sea stars do not resemble the trepang at all, but they are closely related animals. There is a great variety in size, colour and form. Typically the sea stars consist of a central body or disc, from which five arms radiate. However, many species have a greater number of arms and some as many as fifty. The sea stars move with the aid of small suction cups on the lower sides of their arms. These cups also serve the purpose of holding and killing corals, shells and other molluscs. Amongst the numerous kinds of often very beautiful sea stars, the crown of thorns *(Acanthaster planci)* has achieved a certain fame in the last decade. It is feared that this coral predator, the population of which 'suddenly' exploded, will destroy large parts of the coral reef, and there are many accounts of reef damage by the crown of thorns from the northern areas of the Barrier Reef. Whether or not the crown of thorns represents a real threat to the reef ecology and its survival, or whether its sudden population explosion merely represents an event in the ecological cycle, has been the subject of heated discussions and controversy in the scientific world. All one can say at this stage is that present knowledge is not sufficient to answer this question, but it seems that the advance of the crown of thorns has slowed down in recent years.

The delicate sea urchins are closely related to the starfish or sea stars and are amongst the most conspicuous animals of the reef. Unlike the sea stars they do not have arms but consist of a round, oval or disc-shaped body which is covered with dense, often spiny, spikes. These spikes are mostly thin and brittle and some contain poisonous substances, so they should not be handled. The most beautiful species probably is the red-coloured slate pencil urchin *(Heterocentrotus mammillatus)* which has numerous blunt flat spikes. Another conspicuous kind is the needle spined urchin *(Diadema setosum),* with its long brittle needle-like sharp spines, which usually have white stripes.

One of the most lasting experiences of one's first reef visit is without doubt the spectacle of a multitude of small, brightly coloured fish that swim through the labyrinth of coral growth without taking any notice of the human invader. The reef fish are small and exceptionally colourful. Nearly every shade of colour, colour combination and pattern is present. The ecological significance of the colour is somewhat of a mystery. It is difficult to see that it would serve as protection or disguise, since the fish contrast sharply with the surroundings. I. Bennett, one of the authorities on reef ecology, considers that the colour may help the individual fish to recognize its own species in the multitude of fish in the coral reef jungle. Another reason may be that the excellent protection and variety of habitats provided by the reef allows natural evolution to experiment wildly, and the chances of survival are high. Whatever the case may be, the association of brightly coloured fish and coral reefs is inseparable and is a characteristic feature all over the tropical world.

The total number of fish species in the Great Barrier Reef is not known with any precision, which is not surprising considering the vast expanse of the reef and the difficulties of exploring it. Over 1400 species have been recorded and the total number is probably considerably higher. In the vicinity of Heron Island alone, which is the best researched coral reef area, 700 fish species have been found.

It is useless to try to list different fish species without illustrations; but two species will find mention here, one because it is most beautiful, the other because it is most dangerous. The butterfly cod with its long, wing-like fins and its colourful body which is characterized by numerous bands of alternating light and dark colour tones is one of the most attractive fish of the reef. In contrast to the majority of reef fish, which live and move in schools, the butterfly cod is an individualist, moving slowly and gracefully through the lagoons and corals.

Also an individualist is the stone fish, which is as ugly as the butterfly cod is beautiful. It rests motionless on the bottom of sandy lagoons or coral pools in anticipation of prey. With its dirty, grey-brown colour and its spiny back the stone fish is well camouflaged and can hardly be seen against the background of sand and coral rocks. This is not only fatal for the unsuspecting little fish that comes too close, but can also be very painful and even fatal to the person that steps on the sharp spines of the fish. Fortunately, injuries can now be successfully treated with an antidote.

Apart from the fish that live in the reef itself and never venture into the open sea, there are of course numerous species of fish which live in the open sea but visit the reef in search for food. These fish are usually larger, and many are popular game fish such as tuna, mackerel, kingfish, queenfish and many others. A less welcome visitor to the reef is the notorious shark which frequents the reef area in search of easy prey. Of all dangers in the reef the shark undoubtedly is the most potent, and shark attacks, which of course are not restricted to the reef area, do occur every year and some are fatal. But again the danger has to be seen in its proper perspective, as the total number of shark fatalities in the last fifty years does not amount to more than fifty, while drowning may claim the same number in one year.

The Great Barrier Reef is a vast natural laboratory, a biological world of wonders in which scientists, lay naturalists and tourists can observe and study the complex relationships of different life forms and the inexhaustible experimentation of evolution with these life forms. The reef represents a relatively stable ecosystem that has survived thousands, even millions of years, in spite of climatic changes, sea level changes and up and down movements of the sea floor.

But suddenly the survival of this ecosystem is threatened by the interference of man. The ever increasing flood of tourists is probably one of the lesser threats, since the access to the majority of reefs is difficult and their great number alone is a certain safeguard. The more frequently visited reefs do, however, clearly show the destruction by man and most visible are the broken pieces of coral, or worse, the overturned boulders that used to serve as homes for a great variety of life forms. Less obvious is the impoverishment of the shell fauna brought about by the ruthless collection of shells which in recent years has become worse with commercial interests entering the field.

A more potent threat to the reef area as a whole is the possibility of an exploitation of its natural resources. The reef with its high production of organic material naturally is a potential source of oil, and borings had already begun but were fortunately stopped because of public pressure. The commercial interests, however, exert strong pressure for the resumption of drilling and this will increase with the coming energy shortages.

The most serious dangers for the reef are the ever increasing pollution of the coastal waters and open ocean and the ever potent threat of oil spills, since these endanger the survival of the very basic components of the reef, the coral.

---

49 Nullarbor Station (Nullarbor Plain) is typical of large but lonely settlements in the arid zone of Australia.

50 Settlements in the arid zone are scarce and widely scattered. The few stations that are viable and have survived droughts and floods are very large and often span thousands of square kilometres of land. Availability of water, above everything else, controls the distribution of stations.

51 No book on Australia is complete without Ayers Rock, the world's largest monolith. Like its eastern and western neighbours, Mt Connor and the Olgas, Ayers Rock is a residual inselberg that has survived the forces of weathering and erosion for millions of years because of its massiveness and resistance. It consists of coarse arkose (a kind of sandstone) and rises 350 m above the plain. Ayers Rock is also a sacred site for the Aborigines and some of the weathering caves at the base contain interesting Aboriginal drawings.

52 The base of the monolith is fretted by numerous caves which, like the rock itself, are millions of years old.

The process forming these caves is probably a kind of salt weathering whereby small platy rock fragments are loosened by recrystallisation of salt. This process seems to start near the base of the rock and then works slowly upwards and inwards into the rock. Some of these caves are 10 metres deep and several tens of metres high.

53 Deep roundish solution pits occur on the upper slopes and the summit area of Ayers Rock. These are due to slow chemical solution of the rock in places where water tends to collect for longer periods.

54 The Olgas, a group of dome-shaped rocky hills in viewing distance of Ayers Rock, also represent residual inselbergs. They consist of massive conglomerate and rise some 500 m above the surrounding plain.

55 The baobab *(Adansonia gregorii)* is one of the most remarkable trees of the tropical north. Its enormous trunk consists of soft wood and contains large amounts of water which permit the tree to survive long periods of drought.

The Economy

The Australian economy is diversified and highly advanced in its structure. Despite the fact that it is the product of the efforts of a relatively very small population of only 14 millions (comparable in number with the population of the Netherlands or of Czechoslovakia), it is a significant source of produce and raw materials in world trade, notably in metallic materials, coal, animal products and grain, and while it provides much of its own requirements for machinery and textiles it also acts as a worthwhile market for the industries of other countries. In carrying out these roles Australia is handicapped by the high costs arising from its distance from the world markets and suppliers, and by the small size and the extreme physical dispersion of its own internal market. Apart from a limited Free Trade Agreement with neighbouring New Zealand, and involvement in long-term marketing contracts for some commodities with overseas companies, Australia is not a member of any economic bloc and buys and sells from all countries. Tariffs are used to protect many local manufacturing activities and are justified on the grounds of high internal costs. Income per capita is $A.4,404 (1975–76).

Australia has come to be known to the outside world largely for its exported products which are generally of rural origin. But the reality of employment structure reflects a different situation, despite major increases in mineral production in recent years. The Australian economy is dominated by commerce, manufacturing and administration, rather than by primary production. Workers in all forms of primary production and in the mining industry together totalled only 462,000 at the 1971 Census, this being 9 per cent of the employed population of 5,240,000 at that time, and well under half those employed in manufacturing (1,216,000), about two thirds the number in the categories of finance, public administration and defence (647,000), and less than half those employed in wholesale and retail trade (988,000). The construction industries and the utilities supplying water, gas and electricity employ significantly more workers (503,000) than the industries that provide the overwhelming bulk of Australia's exports. This configuration of the economic structure underlies and makes possible the distinctive geographical distribution pattern of the Australian population, with only 14 per cent of the total living in situations described as rural, and more than 64 per cent in cities greater than 100,000.

A major preoccupation of the Australian economy is its struggle to overcome the problems created by space and excessive distances, to knit together the Australian society across the immensity of land that it occupies so thinly and to overcome 'the tyranny of distance'. The territory used by the 14 million Australians is comparable with the United States of America without Alaska, or all of Europe from the Atlantic in the west to a line joining the Caspian and White Seas in the east. Although some 30 per cent of this territory of 7.678 million square kilometres is not effectively occupied, being in the main arid desert, the remainder must be

Values are shown in terms of Australian dollars ($)

		1965–66	1973–74	1974–75	1975–76
Domestic product and national expenditure					
Gross Domestic Product (GDP)	$m	20,545	50,703	59,987	70,243
Personal consumption expenditure	,,	12,922	29,274	35,143	41,543
Food and drink	,,	4,105	7,974	9,231	10,819
Household durables	,,	973	2,484	3,050	3,788
Travel and communication	,,	1,847	4,378	5,346	6,372
Gross fixed capital expenditure	,,	5,709	11,909	14,332	16,721
Private	,,	3,657	7,947	8,726	10,323
Public authorities	,,	2,052	3,962	5,606	6,398
Gross farm product	,,	1,913	4,479	3,622	3,727
GDP at 1966–67 prices	,,	21,214	32,502	32,703	33,216
GDP per head (at current prices)	$	1,771	3,821	4,454	5,161

Overseas trade					
Total exports. f.o.b.	$m	2,721	6,910	8,726	9,606
Total imports, f.o.b.	,,	2,939	6,085	8,080	8,240
Percentage of total exports to Japan	%	10.3	31.2	28.2	32.9
Percentage of total exports to U.K.	,,	28.0	6.6	5.5	4.2
Percentage of total exports to U.S.A.	,,	25.9	10.9	9.5	10.1
Percentage of total imports from Japan	,,	16.0	17.8	17.6	19.5
Percentage of total imports from U.K.	,,	16.1	13.9	15.0	13.4
Percentage of total imports from U.S.A.	,,	11.5	22.2	20.7	20.1
Major export commodities, f.o.b.					
Wool (greasy)	$m	700	1,062	664	842
Meat (fresh, chilled, frozen)	,,	262	761	418	634
Wheat	,,	264	517	1,028	921
Machinery and transport equipment	,,	116	446	565	496
Iron ore and concentrates	,,	3	499	706	771
Coal, coke and briquettes	,,	63	348	733	1,036
Sugar	,,	94	223	645	570
Major import commodities, f.o.b.					
Machinery (non-electrical)	,,	566	888	1,358	1,339
Road motor vehicles	,,	237	506	778	864
Petroleum and petroleum products	,,	252	377	722	806

From: Australia 1977 at a Glance

interconnected and the desert must be spanned to effect the necessary linkages. These tasks directly absorb the efforts of 7 per cent of the total workforce, engaged in the transport and communication industries, and the magnitude of the effort involved, and its ramifications throughout the entire economic fabric, are clearly shown by other statistics. The Australian railnet exceeds 42,000 km in track length, 40,000 of which is under government management, and annually shifts more than 200 million tonnes of freight. There are 86 government-operated aerodromes and an additional 362 licensed landing fields which together handled 9.3 million paying passengers on internal flights in 1975–76, and 1.5 million overseas passengers. The average Australian flies once every 16 months; if his journey is within Australia, it will average 803 km in distance, and if to a destination beyond the national boundaries he will fly on average 7080 km to reach it. The 845,000 km of roads, a quarter of which are bitumen-sealed, are used by 6,365,000 motor vehicles and 296,000 motor cycles (1976) and about 600,000 new vehicles appear on the roads each year of which 420,000 are produced locally.

The magnitude of the Australian achievement in overcoming the hindrance of excessive distance and in tapping the continental resources for the benefit of the local community and the wider world are indicated by her pattern of international trade. Exports in 1975–76 totalled $9,556 million, with the internal breakdown of this figure indicating positive relative advantage especially in the areas of mineral and farm production: vegetable and animal-based food products provided $3,160 million (33 per cent) of all exports, with cereals ($1,377 million), meat and animals ($698 million), and sugar ($585 million) being the major items. Inedible crude materials of mine and field origin yielded 27 per cent of exports, and were dominated by textile fibres, mainly wool ($977 million), and metal ores and scrap, mainly iron ore and bauxite ($1,312 million). Mineral fuels contributed 12 per cent of exports, notably from coal ($981 million) and Australia is one of the few industrialized countries to experience a favourable trade balance in the energy field, with exports exceeding imports by $336 million in 1975–76.

The pattern of import trade indicates the areas of relative deficit in Australian industrial production. $8,240 million were spent on imports in 1975–76, the largest general area being the $3,177 million (39 per cent) spent on machinery and transport equipment, a figure far exceeding the $496 million of Australian exports in these items. Other manufactured goods imported totalled $2,510 million (30 per cent), with major items in textiles and clothing ($793 million), fine instruments ($274 million) and paper products ($186 million); in the 'other manufactures' category, imports to Australia exceeded exports from Australia ($1,234 million) by $2,276 million. Imports and exports of chemicals were more evenly balanced, reflecting the elaboration of the Australian industrial structure during recent decades, and imports of $710 millions were not greatly in excess of the $646

Agriculture		1965–66	1973–74	1974–75	1975–76
Gross value of primary production	$m	n.a.	6,715	6,202	6,605
Crops	,,	n.a.	2,846	3,193	3,234
Livestock slaughtering, etc.	,,	n.a.	1,696	1,019	1,291
Livestock products	,,	n.a.	1,859	1,655	1,700
Forestry, fishing and hunting	,,	n.a.	314	334	379
Output					
Wheat	'000 tonnes	7,067	11,987	11,357	11,982
Wool	m kg	754	701	793	754
Meat	'000 tonnes	1,690	1,978	2,229	2,600

Mining production					
Value added	$m	441	2,001	2,650	3,070
Output					
Metallic content of minerals					
Copper	'000 tonnes	92	257	236	218
Lead	,,	368	380	417	397
Zinc	,,	355	445	508	479
Iron	,,	4,366	58,218	60,860	58,263
Bauxite	,,	1,186	18,642	22,205	n.a.
Black coal	,,	31,942	59,478	70,142	69,269
Crude oil	'000 cu m	..	23,162	23,096	23,839
Natural gas	mil cu m	4	4,403	4,633	5,172

Manufacturing					
Value added	$m	–	13,149	15,241	
Metal products, transport equipment, machinery, etc.	,,	n.a.	5,529	6,628	
Food, beverages, tobacco	,,	n.a.	2,126	2,651	
Textiles, clothing, footwear	,,	n.a.	1,157	1,106	
Paper and products, printing	,,	n.a.	1,111	1,279	
Chemicals, petroleum products	,,	n.a.	1,076	1,173	
Output					
Ingot steel	'000 tonnes	5,650	7,504	7,856	7,937
Cement	,,	3,747	5,412	5,273	5,007
Beer	m litres	1,271	1,868	1,954	1,932
Tobacco and cigarettes	m kg	25.4	31.4	31.0	31.1
Cars and station wagons	'000	294	382	377	369
Electricity output	m kWh	38,279	69,743	73,933	76,597

From: Australia 1977 at a Glance

million exports, although the tendency is for Australia to export elements and compounds, and to import more sophisticated chemical materials.

A Radical Reorientation

During the past 25 years there has been a radical reorientation of Australian trade affiliation. As recently as 1953–54 Great Britain supplied Australia with 49 per cent of her imports and took 36 per cent of her exports, and the other (present day) major European Economic Community partners contributed 9 per cent of Australian imports and took 23 per cent of her exports. By contrast, at this time Japan's share was less than one per cent of imports and a modest 7 per cent of exports, and the United States provided 11 per cent of imports and received 7 per cent of Australian exports. In 1975–76 Britain provided under 14 per cent of imports and 4 per cent of Australian exports, and the other major E.E.C. partners had remained static as suppliers of 9 per cent of Australian imports and had slumped to only 11 per cent of exports. Japan, by contrast, had experienced major gains, taking 33 per cent of Australia's exports and supplying 20 per cent of her imports; the United States, while remaining steady at over 10 per cent of exports, now provided 20 per cent of Australian imports. The rise of Japan, as customer and supplier, and as competitor with Australian exporters of manufactured goods to the neighbouring South East Asia and Pacific Island markets, has inexorably replaced Europe as the focus of Australian trade relations.

Although the balance of payments on commodity flows is substantially in favour of Australia, this advantage is more than offset by transactions outside the commodity area, so that in 1975–76 the overall balance on current account showed a deficit of $840 million. In the non-commodity area the major items in which Australia expended more than she received were for transportation ($534 millions of excess expenditure), for property income ($909 million), and for travel ($292 million). The normal expectation in Australia throughout the postwar period has been that balance of payments deficits will be more than compensated by inflows of outside capital which have generally been readily forthcoming and directed especially to funding expansions in Australian manufacturing and mining industries. The steady growth of the Australian economy since 1945, which has been particularly associated with the success of the immigration program and the exploitation of the newly discovered and very large deposits of iron ore, bauxite and coal in a context of political stability, has made Australia an attractive field for foreign investment. This attractiveness has been enhanced by the determination of successive Australian governments since Federation to offer substantial tariff protection to domestic manufactures and thus to welcome the capital needed to produce goods in Australia rather than to welcome these same goods, produced very likely by the same companies, imported from overseas.

Considerations of protecting 'infant industries' still remain the basis for protectionism. Also, the extreme dispersion of the Australian market together with its small size impose fundamental costs of a high order on manufacturers seeking to achieve a national distribution of their goods and give further justification. Added to these considerations is the experience gained in two world wars, that Australia needs a firm industrial base for its own physical protection.

Despite the general agreement that Australian industries merit assistance, there is continuing debate on the levels of support and the types of industries that should be supported. Australia's contribution to world trade could as easily be made simply by the present workforce employed in its rural, mining and processing industries, but the realities of internal politics insure that no government will move to dismantle the industrial structure that has evolved and that gives employment to a quarter of all Australians; rationalization of the structure is possible only in sectors where costs of production in Australia are quite drastically and demonstrably out of line with costs in foreign countries. An Industries Assistance Commission advises the Government on relative costs of Australian as compared with foreign production, and recommends appropriate levels of assistance; if Government finds the costs too high to be politically acceptable it has the power to cripple an industry by reducing levels of assistance. This step has recently been taken with the shipbuilding industry, and it is clear that the textile industry is currently under heavy threat from the expanding manufactures of southern Asia. Australia is coming to realise that high tariff levels designed to protect local employment can generate hostility in neighbouring countries seeking outlets in foreign markets for their own fledgling industries.

The industrial structure that has evolved under these circumstances is surprisingly diverse. For example, in 1975–76 Australia produced 30 million pairs of footwear, 4 million electric motors, 533,000 television sets, 7.9 million tonnes of steel, 422,000 motor vehicles and 744,000 tonnes of paper.

Many of the basic material resources necessary for further economic growth are abundantly available within Australia. Despite continual problems arising from climatic unreliability she is able to supply large, if irregular surpluses of foodstuffs to world markets each year. Australian reserves of iron ore and bauxite are the largest yet discovered, her supply of recoverable coal is large by any standard and her deep-lying coal beds are estimated in terms of millions of millions of tonnes. The extent of gas supplies on the extensive continental shelf are known to be substantial even at this early stage of exploration, and her resources of uranium ore are estimated at one fifth of the world total. Australia has never hesitated to share her abundant resource supplies with the outside world, but this policy has resulted in relatively high incomes for her people, and this in turn has led to high costs of production in all activities in which a significant labour component is necessary. The only really 'successful' Australian industries, that is, industries able to compete on world markets, are those in which it has been possible to reduce the labour component of costs to levels well below those prevailing elsewhere in the world, most notably in mining and in farm production, both of these being areas susceptible to high levels of mechanization. Australia's economic future is bright, but it is not free of problems.

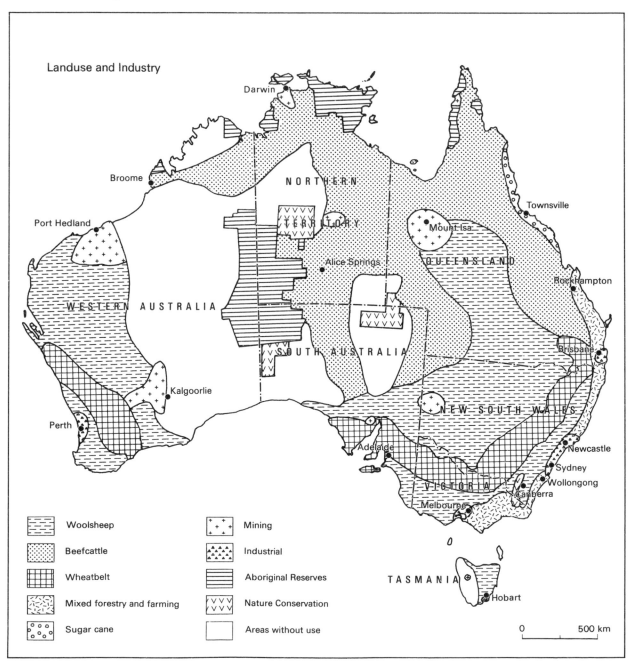

Landuse and Industry

	Woolsheep		Mining
	Beefcattle		Industrial
	Wheatbelt		Aboriginal Reserves
	Mixed forestry and farming		Nature Conservation
	Sugar cane		Areas without use

0   500 km

56 Bushfires are a common feature of the dry Australian environment and cause heavy losses of live stock and grazing land every year. Although many fires are caused through human negligence, many others start by natural causes. There is little doubt that fires have been with the Australian environment for a long time and many plants show a surprising adaptation and resistance to fire. The Aborigines used fire for hunting.

57 Flooding is another hazard common to the Australian environment and here, too, certain environments are well adapted, such as these red river gums in the flood plain of the Murray River, which tolerate prolonged annual flooding.

58 The trees are, however, not able to survive permanent flooding caused by man-made structures. Here the construction of a dam has drowned the flood plain area and the trees are gradually dying.

59 The Murray-Murrumbidgee irrigation scheme is, in spite of certain difficulties associated with salting and a rising water table, a most successful piece of irrigation engineering. Water from the reservoirs is taken in broad long channels across the Riverina and distributed over the riverine plain, on both sides of the Murray, making the area one of the most intensively used and most productive agricultural regions of Australia.

60 This aerial view of Wangaratta is typical of the eastern parts of the Riverina. The river courses form wide meanders some of which are cut through resulting in the formation of oxbows. Old, completely abandoned river courses can be easily traced because of the vegetation pattern associated with them. The photograph is taken in a drought period.

61 Flooding and drought are two natural hazards the Australian farmer has to live with no matter where his farm is located. Here the flood is covering large areas of agricultural land near the Dandenongs and only the trees fringing the river course give an indication of its location.

62 In the arid zone surface water is insufficient to permit cultivation of crops and underground water therefore has to be used to irrigate the fields. The fields stand in striking contrast to the dry surroundings.

63 Some parts of Victoria are similar to European landscapes because of the intensive land use pattern and the small size of the fields.

64 The southeast of South Australia is one of the most productive areas of the State. Not only does it provide excellent pasture land and good land for wheat production, but also some of the best land for the establishment of pine plantations. The vicinity of Mt Gambier, which is shown here, is one of the largest pine producing areas in Australia. A newly established pine plantation can be seen in the centre left.

65 The Australian farmer must be rugged and must be able to cope not only with a great variety of work but also with years of drought and flooding as well as with an ever changing agricultural market.

66 Paddy melons are a common sight along the roadside in the arid zone. The melons are not native to Australia but were introduced by the Afghans during the construction of the telegraph line.

67 Australian wines are of excellent quality and are enjoying an ever increasing popularity. The centre of Australian wine making is the Barossa Valley, but other areas such as McLaren Vale, Clare, Rutherglen and the Hunter Valley are also important wine producing centres.

68 Australia's vast agricultural areas demand mechanisation and the viability of its agricultural economy depends very much on the efficiency of machines like this cotton harvester.

69 Monocultures like cotton are very vulnerable to disease and pests and the application of pesticides is necessary to maintain high yields. One of the common cotton pests is the cotton harlequin bug *(Tectowris diophthalamus)*.

70–Sugar is the most important product of the coastal
72 areas of the tropical north of Australia and, in fact, represents the third most important agricultural export product after wool and meat. The production of sugar is, of course, highly mechanised from planting to harvesting and processing, but the industry is still relatively labour intensive particularly at harvest time.

73 Sheep have for a long time represented the symbol and guarantee of Australia's wealth and prosperity. Although wool has been replaced by minerals as the main export, it is still the most important agricultural export. The future of the wool industry now looks much brighter than it did in the early seventies when it experienced its worst slump ever.

74 The stockman is Australia's equivalent to the 'cowboy' and he is much romanticised in songs and stories. The daring horse-riding stockman is, however, slowly becoming a feature of the past and much of the mustering today is done by motor bike, four-wheel drive vehicle or even by helicopter.

57 58

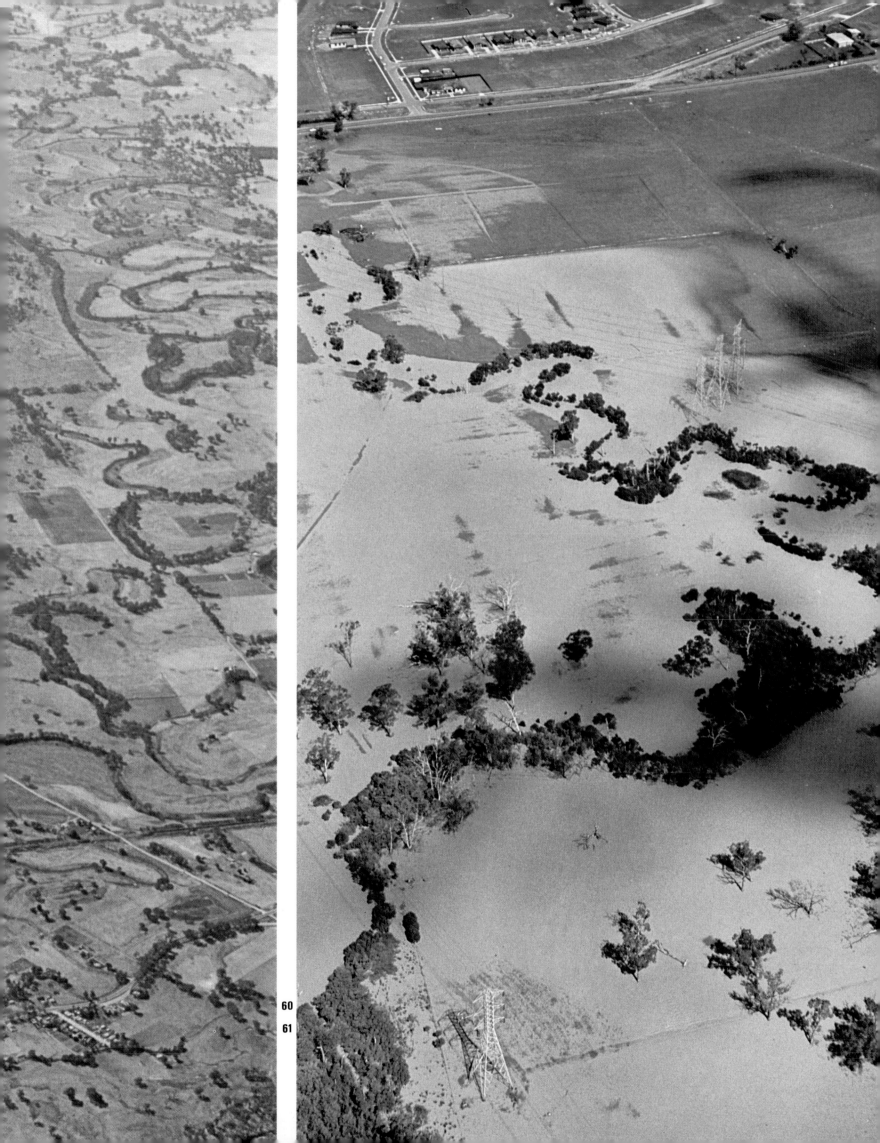

67

66

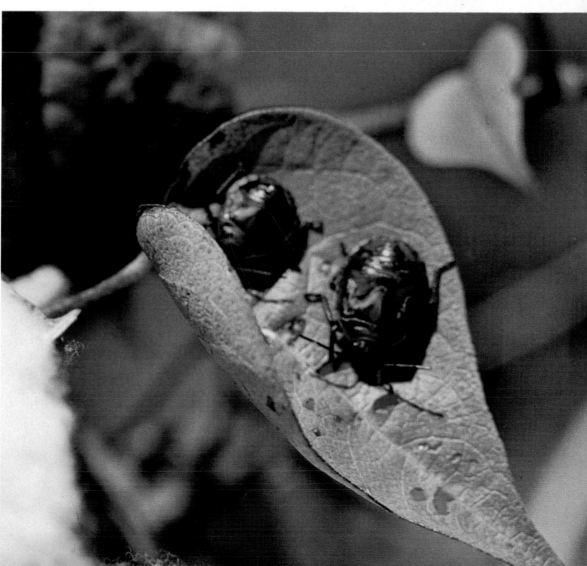

68
69

Australia's History before Colonization

Because of its isolation, the Australian continent's human occupation came relatively late. It was probably during the last ice age that the vast continent was settled by dark-skinned people who originated in Asia. Their immigration started about 40,000 years ago, possibly earlier, when the sea level was considerably lower than today and land bridges connected several islands of the Indonesian Archipelago. In spite of this, the newcomers had to cross a number of deep and relatively extensive straits. They did not appear to possess any seaworthy crafts nor any navigation skills and it is therefore likely that they arrived in small groups on primitive rafts and more by luck than intention. These original Australians or Aborigines were nomadic hunters, fishermen and gatherers, and they gradually spread over the entire continent, including the island of Tasmania which, at the time, was connected with the mainland by a land bridge. The Australian Aborigines maintained this nomadic life style until the arrival of the Europeans, and some small groups in the remote areas of the interior continue it to this day.

With the melting of the great ice masses of the northern hemisphere from about 16,000 years ago, the sea level gradually rose and many of the land bridges became submerged, so that movement across the Indonesian Archipelago became increasingly difficult and migration eventually ceased altogether.

The access to Australia over the open sea could, from then on, only be achieved by a seafaring people with enough knowledge in navigation to dare the voyage into the unknown. The advance of the Malay people into the Indonesian Archipelago some 4000 years ago did not reach New Guinea or Australia probably because of the effective water barriers. Later expansion of other cultures like the Chinese, South Indian Hindus and Buddhists or Muslim traders failed because of political or military upheavals in their home countries.

The inhabitants of the neighbouring Indonesian Archipelago were mostly sailing their crafts close to the coast and did not venture into the open sea. One exception were the people of Macassar in Celebes, who were experienced sailors and specialized in the collection and transport of trepang *(bêche-de-mer)*, which was much sought after in China, where it was regarded as a delicacy and aphrodisiac. From the eighteenth century onwards their small fleets frequented the northern shores of Australia in their search for trepang, which they also processed at these coasts. They arrived with the north-west monsoon and left with the onset of south-east trade winds.

The collection of trepang by foreigners did not affect the Aboriginal economy, as it was not known to the natives as a food source. There was also little social contact between them and the Macassar people. Occasionally conflicts flared up because the presence of the trepang collectors and their camps on the land were considered as infringements of tribal territories. The Aborigines of Cape York on the northern tip of the north coast also had periodic contact with foreign people. Between Cape York and New Guinea a number of islands rise from the shallow Torres Strait and the inhabitants of Papua occasionally reached the Australian mainland with their large sailing rafts. It has remained a mystery why this contact did not lead to an introduction into Australia of agricultural practices which were relatively highly developed in New Guinea and which were adapted by the inhabitants of the Torres Strait islands. It must be one of the great ironies in the history of mankind that Australia was not colonized from neighbouring Melanesia, Indonesia or from the relatively nearby Asiatic continent, but by a people who lived at the other end of the world.

In the Middle Ages, the old Greek saga of a rich southland in the Indian Ocean was revived. Hopes for its eventual discovery received a boost with the discovery of new sea routes to the far east and, of course, the discovery of the American continent. Finally, there was the proof by Magellan's voyage of the global shape of the earth and the interconnection of the Indian and Pacific Oceans. It was assumed that in the vastness of these oceans there had to be a 'terra australis' as a kind of counterbalance to the landmasses of the northern hemisphere continents. In the sixteenth century Spanish and Portuguese seafarers tried to find this mysterious 'terra australis' by sailing the Pacific westward from South America; yet they failed because the strong westerly trades drove them north-west and they finally reached the spice islands, and Torres even passed the strait named after him, sailing close to the south coast of New Guinea without seeing the Australian continent to the south of his route.

Holland, which had established its supremacy over the spice islands in 1602 with the foundation of the Netherlands East India Trading Company, also sent its ships to search for 'terra australis' and finally, in 1606, the Dutchman Willem Jansz landed on the western shores of Cape York Peninsula and thus became the first European to set foot on Australian soil. He did not find any of the expected rich treasures, but instead was confronted by 'cruel black savages' who in his opinion possessed none of the attributes of civilization and obviously lived a most miserable life. In the following forty years Dutch seafarers sailed along and mapped the entire north, west and south coasts of the continent which, quite inappropriately, they named 'New Holland'. Their reports about the inhospitable dry coast and uncivilized natives remained negative and so the Dutch interest in the new continent eventually ceased altogether.

The British did not show any serious interest in the Pacific area until the second half of the eighteenth century. They, too, had high hopes of discovering the mysterious rich southern continent, and the discovery of Tahiti in 1767 by the Englishman Wallis gave this hope new impetus. In 1768 the British Government therefore decided to send a most generously equipped expedition into this area. Officially the expedition's task was the observation of the Venus transit between sun and earth from Tahiti. However the commander of the ship *Endeavour,* James Cook, had a second, secret mission, which was the search for 'terra australis'. After months of futile tacking in the vastness of the Pacific, Cook decided to abandon this plan and set sail towards New Zealand, which had been discovered in 1642 by Abel Tasman. From there he wanted to investigate the unknown east coast of New Holland. Cook's decision led to the discovery of the attractive, well-watered and densely forested east coast and with it he laid the foundation for the future colonization of Australia.

Before Cook left Australian waters he declared Britain's sovereignty over the entire eastern seaboard, which he named New South Wales. In the following decade Cook was sent on two further expeditions into the Pacific, which he traversed from South America to New Zealand, from North America to China, and from the Bering Strait in the north to the Antarctic waters in the south, without finding any trace of the mysterious 'terra australis'. He had proved its non-existence once and for all and had returned it to the world of legends.

The discovery and exploration of the east coast of Australia did not raise much enthusiasm or even interest in England and Cook therefore never received full credit for his achievements in his lifetime. England was preoccupied at the time with the independence movement and, eventually, the Independence War of the North American colonies. Their final loss in 1783 proved to be of vital influence in the future of Australia.

By losing the American colonies England had not only been deprived of a rich trading area but also of its dumping ground for undesirable convicts. In the years following the American independence the prisons in the large cities and the convict ships on the Thames and other rivers became increasingly overcrowded, and the inhuman conditions in these prisons led to rebellions and eventually to political strife in Parliament.

To relieve the potentially dangerous situation, the King, in 1787, announced a plan in Parliament to send convicts to New South Wales, where a new colony was to be founded. In May the same year, Arthur Phillip was given command of the first convict fleet and received orders to establish a convict colony at Botany Bay, which had been recommended by James Cook as a favourable site for a settlement. It seems that the deportation of convicts was not the only reason for Britain's sudden interest in the Pacific area. Political and strategic considerations, particularly in view of France's expansion in the area, probably played a major role, although this was never officially admitted.

Phillip's fleet consisted of eleven ships and over 1000 men and women, three-quarters of whom were convicts. In January 1788 the fleet arrived at Botany Bay, but this site did not appear to be as suitable as expected and Phillip decided to establish the settlement in the excellent natural port of Port Jackson, a little north of Botany Bay. The new settlement was named Sydney Cove and with its establishment the modern history of Australia began.

History and Politics of Modern Australia

The history of modern Australia is short and may appear uneventful if one draws a comparison with the hectic and troubled history of Europe. This is because it never was a significant military or political power, nor did it occupy a geographic position which would have brought it into the sphere of conflict of other nations. The decisive years of Australian political development, in fact most of its entire history, took place under the umbrella of British protection without fear of militant neighbours, but also without great internal conflicts brought about by different ethnic or religious groups or by warlike natives. The history of Australia is therefore one of internal politics and of struggles for influence and power in colonial and later state affairs.

The first, and so far only, foreign attack on Australian soil took place during the second world war by the Japanese, and this led to a sudden and profound change in Australia's strategic and political alignment. From this time Australia looked to the United States of America for protection and security, since Great Britain was no longer in a position to guarantee it.

The second world war brought about another important change in the composition of the population. Until then the people had been almost entirely of British stock. Culture, language, tradition and customs were British, with some local modifications. The great influx of non-British migrants in the aftermath of the war brought about significant changes in many attitudes and values of Australians, and a general opening up of the society.

Australia's modern history begins with the landing on 26 January 1788 of Governor Phillip and his fleet on the shores of Sydney Cove. The first years of the convict settlement were hard and difficult and there was an early constant shortage of food and other essential supplies. The convicts nearly all originated from the slums of London or other British cities and so did not possess the knowledge or ability, nor indeed the inclination, to work on the land. This was aggravated in the early years by the fact that the European seeds that had been brought into the new colony failed to germinate. It took, therefore, a considerable time for the colony to become reasonably self-sufficient in basic foodstuffs. Slowly the colony grew and its economy received a tremendous boost with the introduction by John Macarthur of Merino sheep at the beginning of the nineteenth century. Within years an excellent wool was produced and eagerly bought by British textile manufacturers. When Governor Macquarie arrived in 1810, the colony was well past its most difficult years and under his strict and stable rule the foundations for future economic prosperity were laid. Macquarie was a keen builder and much of Sydney's basic street design still bears his mark. He also initiated the construction of many buildings, some of which are still standing today, like the St James Church in Sydney or the St Matthews Church in Windsor. More important, however, was his attitude towards the population, in particular his fairness and lack of prejudice in dealing with ex-convicts and their descendants, known then as emancipists. Macquarie was the first governor who clearly recognized the contribution of the emancipists to the advancement of the colony and he openly acknowledged this and sponsored them wherever it was appropriate and deserved. His main architect, Francis Greenway, for instance, was an ex-convict who had been transported to Australia for forgery. Macquarie's support for the emancipists did not meet with much approval among the free settlers, who feared that their monopoly in economic and social affairs was endangered. Macquarie did not manage to close the gap between the two social classes; his pro-emancipist stand probably worsened the situation and, in fact, the infuriated free settlers and their chief spokesman Macarthur became instrumental in his recall in 1822. Among the emancipists, however, Macquarie is remembered as a man who, for the first time, gave them the feeling of pride and confidence in themselves, in their achievements and their new country. For them he was 'the prince of men, Australia's pride and joy'.

The period between 1820 and 1850 witnessed a constant expansion of the colony. New grazing country was discovered west of the divide and in the south and west of the continent new colonies were established. At the same time, there was some political progress aimed at partial self-government. Also significant was the end of convict transportation in 1840 to New South Wales and in 1851 to Tasmania.

The settlement of South Australia began in 1836 when a small group of idealistic settlers landed in the vicinity of Adelaide. It was founded as a province by free settlers, not as a convict settlement, a fact which South Australians even today are quick to point out. The settlers of the new province originated from the industrious, serious-minded middle class of England and few were without financial means or without a trade or commercial knowledge. Their aim was to establish a new, stable and prosperous society. The natural environment was favourable. The foreland of the Mt Lofty Ranges provided relatively fertile soils and the rainfall proved to be reasonably reliable. Transport problems were also initially minimal since the deep Spencer and St Vincent Gulfs allowed ships to sail virtually to the farms' doorsteps. The prosperity and stability of South Australia from the beginning of its history is well expressed in the solid stone buildings the settlers erected.

Even stables and shearing sheds were built of stone; everything was built to last since the settlers had come to stay and to make the country their new homeland. The rich grazing country of Victoria was discovered in the 1830s by squatters who had come from Van Diemen's Land (Tasmania) where grazing land had already become scarce. The first settlements were undertaken without official approval, but once the news of its great grazing potential had been spread it attracted great numbers of free settlers. Then official sanction was given and in 1850 'Australia Felix', as the new district was known, was declared a new, separate colony.

In Queensland too, squatters initially occupied the land illegally and were the forerunners of the future settlement. In 1824 the convict station at the mouth of the Brisbane River was founded and this soon served as a centre from which squatters spread inland. By 1840, they had already moved stock over the Great Divide westward and settlement was soon officially sanctioned. By that time the most fertile areas, the Darling Downs, had been occupied. In 1859 Queensland was declared a separate colony, independent from New South Wales.

The remoteness, isolation and aridity of Western Australia were the main reasons for the lack of interest in its occupation. It was only in 1826 that Western Australia was officially annexed by the British Crown, primarily to forestall any foreign, particularly French, claims to the unoccupied land. To manifest this claim, a small group of soldiers and convicts was landed at the south coast, and laid the foundations for the present township of Albany. Three years later the Swan River settlement was founded with substantial support from England, but success was not forthcoming. The majority of the free labourers who were brought to Western Australia by English financiers soon disappeared from this barren district to the much more promising and prosperous eastern colonies. The lack of workers became so serious that the survival of the settlement was under threat and the settlers asked the British Government to relieve the labour shortage by sending convicts. The convicts promptly arrived, since transportation to the eastern colonies had already ceased; and between 1850 and 1868, when the last convict ship arrived on Australian shores, a total of 10,000 men and women were landed and made a significant contribution to the Western Australian economy. Real progress, however, was only achieved towards the end of the century when gold was discovered, which led to a rapid inflow of people and capital. The isolation of Western Australia has remained until today, an important factor in the Australian economic and political life in spite of the steadily improving connections by air, rail and road, and it is for this reason that calls for a separation of Western Australia from the Commonwealth find many supporters.

The interior was rapidly opened up by squatters following hard on the heels of exploratory expeditions. After the important crossing of the Blue Mountains in 1813 by G. Blaxland and W.C. Wentworth, expeditions followed one another in quick succession. The river systems of the Murrumbidgee and Murray were explored by C. Sturt in 1830 and he succeeded in following the Murray to its mouth and established that it flowed into the sea, and not to an inland lake. In later expeditions he advanced well into the arid desert area, discovered Cooper Creek and reached the fringes of the Simpson Desert, where he was forced to return. E. J. Eyre, who must have been one of the toughest explorers, made several attempts to advance into the interior but eventually he turned west and walked from Fowlers Bay in South Australia over the desolate Nullarbor Plain to Albany in Western Australia.

The best known and most publicized expedition is the tragic journey of R. O'Hara Burke and W. J. Wills, who tried to cross the continent from south to north. The huge, lavishly equipped expedition was troubled from the start with supply and personnel difficulties. The impatient and inexperienced Burke left his depot at Cooper Creek to push northward with a small team of men, before the rest of the equipment and team had arrived there. He reached the Gulf of Carpentaria, but when he returned to Cooper Creek he found that the camp had been vacated the very same morning. Burke and Wills soon died of exhaustion and hunger, but a third member of the team, King, survived with the help of natives and was found a few months later by a rescue expedition.

A tragic end also came to the German L. Leichhardt, who explored the north of the country. In 1844–45 he successfully explored the country between the Darling Downs and Arnhem Land but, when he tried to traverse the continent from east to west, he never returned and no trace of him has ever been found.

One of the most remarkable Australian explorers was John McDouall Stuart, who was the first white man to reach the centre of Australia and to cross it successfully from south to north. In marked contrast to the generously equipped and financed expeditions of Sturt and of Burke and Wills, Stuart had to be content with modest support. He was an excellent, experienced bushman and the fact that he never lost a man speaks for itself. He led three expeditions into the interior, always with only a team of two men, and he relied solely on horses. During each expedition he pushed further north until eventually, in 1862, he reached the north coast in the vicinity of the present Darwin. His expedition was vital for the construction of the Overland Telegraph line, which approximately followed his route and was completed only ten years later.

The last of the great Australian explorers was E. Giles, who had the ambitious aim to explore the country between the Indian Ocean and the Telegraph line. After several attempts, he finally succeeded in 1875–76 to reach the Telegraph line and then, in an incredible move, turned back and crossed the country again along a more southerly route. Giles never received the fame of other explorers before him, and his fantastic achievements were soon forgotten for he did not discover any fertile land, but rather confirmed that the western part of the continent was a vast sand desert unfit for any agricultural use.

The discovery of gold in New South Wales in February 1851 and a few months later in Victoria resulted in a rush to the goldfields, which initially had disastrous consequences for Australia's traditional economy. Labourers, tradesmen, clerks and even policemen abandoned their jobs and joined the gold rush. The situation worsened when overseas gold seekers arrived in large numbers, putting additional strain on the already decimated police force and other public institutions. In spite of this, Australian goldfields never experienced the lawlessness and rioting which was common on the Californian goldfields a few years earlier. The reason was probably the much stricter organization of the Australian public administration and the fact that the goldfields were situated reasonably close to larger, well-established centres such as Ballarat or Bathurst.

The scene at the Eureka Stockade, Ballarat when troops and miners clashed in the early hours of Sunday, December 3, 1854. Australian Information Service photograph by Don Edwards (reproduced from the Latrobe State Library of Victoria) Historical Scenes

There was, however, one riot, the Eureka Stockade, the first and so far only larger civil disturbance in Australian history. The reasons for the riot were twofold; first there was a general dissatisfaction and disappointment because of the steadily declining gold findings, and secondly there was increasing hatred for the police forces because of their rough methods of collecting taxes in so-called 'licence hunts', at a time when only a small number of diggers found enough gold to pay for the licence.

In Ballarat the situation came to boiling point towards the end of 1854 when the gold diggers formed a 'reform league', the stated aims of which, apart from demands to ease the taxes, were universal male suffrage, vote by secret ballot, and other 'radical' political demands. Provoked by a licence hunt, some of the more radical diggers took up arms and positioned themselves behind a hurriedly erected stockade on a hill overlooking Ballarat. The riot did not last two days. In the early morning of 3 December, troops and police attacked the stockade, which fell within minutes; but twenty-five gold diggers and four soldiers lost their lives.

Another significant event connected with the goldrush was the arrival of large numbers of Chinese and the development of a strong anti-Chinese sentiment, not only among the gold diggers but among the white community as a whole. This sentiment eventually found its official seal with the 'White Australia Policy' (Commonwealth Immigration Restriction Act 1901).

In spite of the difficulties brought about by the sudden influx of people during the goldrush years, the long term effect on the economy was very favourable. In ten years the population nearly trebled, from 400,000 to 1,150,000. More important than the numbers of the newcomers was the fact that most of them possessed skills in trade or commerce and they therefore filled an important gap in the population composition – the middle class. At the same time they brought with them new ideas and attitudes, particularly in the political sphere, and became instrumental in the rapidly increasing demand for internal self-government of the colonies. They also contributed substantially to an improvement in the cultural life of the Australian colonies.

In the years following the goldrush all colonies except Western Australia were granted virtual control over their internal affairs. In 1856 South Australians elected their first parliament, which was based on general male suffrage and secret ballot. The other colonies soon followed. The political achievements were matched by steady economic progress leading to a level of prosperity which was not restricted to the rich squatters and graziers on the land or the bankers and businessmen in the city, but which affected the population at large. The prosperity of Australia was further strengthened by the discovery in 1883 of huge silver, lead and zinc deposits in Broken Hill and the copper ore bodies of Queenstown in Tasmania.

Shortly before the turn of the century, the economic progress came to a sudden halt when world prices for wool, wheat and most metals fell and British financiers abruptly withdrew their capital. Strikes also flared up and even though they all ended with the defeat of the strikers they were important in laying the foundations for an organized political labour movement.

In the centre of political development in the last decade of the nineteenth century were the discussions about the federation of the six Australian States. Since the middle of the century the possibilities of a federation were mentioned now and then by politicians, but there was little response or enthusiasm. In 1891, however, the federation issue gained popularity and momentum with a series of conventions. Little progress was made initially and many delegates, particularly from the smaller States, remained lukewarm to the idea of federation. The biggest problem in bringing the States together in a federation was the difficulty of compromising

Circular Quay, Sydney – date unknown but believed to be between 1870–1880.
Australian Information Service photograph by courtesy Maritime Services Board of N.S.W. Historical Scenes

the interests and rights of the individual States with the demands imposed by a Westminster-type central government. There was also fear among the less populous States that they would become dominated by the two 'giants', New South Wales and Victoria, which between them had two-thirds of the entire population. A compromise was finally achieved with a constitution that was based on the establishment of two Houses, a House of Representatives elected on universal direct suffrage, and a Senate consisting of equal numbers of senators for each State. The Australian Constitution is often described as a mixture of the British and American Constitutions. The House of Representatives is the seat of government and is similar to the British House of Commons. The representatives are elected through universal suffrage by secret ballot and the country is subdivided into electorates of roughly equal numbers of voters. The Senate is a States House; the senators are also elected in free, secret ballots but each State is represented by the same number of senators. This means, of course, that the population of small States has a disproportionally large representation in the Senate.

Two peculiarities of the Australian voting system are the compulsory voting and the so-called preferential voting. Preferential voting means that the voter has to give *all* candidates on his ballot paper a number according to his preference. If no candidate receives an absolute majority of first votes, the 'preferential votes' of the candidate with the least number of first votes are distributed amongst the other candidates. If there is still no absolute majority the preferential votes of the second last candidate are distributed and so on until an absolute majority is achieved. It is therefore not surprising that counting of votes can last over a week if the outcome of an election is close.

The Constitution was not the only hotly discussed federation issue. The choice of a capital was also much debated, for neither Sydney nor Melbourne would allow her rival to be crowned capital. A section was therefore included in the constitution which read: 'The seat of government should be in Commonwealth territory, not less than 100 square miles [260 square kilometres] in area situated within the state of New South Wales not less than 100 miles [160 kilometres] from Sydney'.

The dispute lasted another eight years until, after a lot of haggling, the site of the present Australian Capital Territory was agreed upon and finally, in 1913, the first buildings were started. Progress was sluggish from the beginning and the little enthusiasm that existed soon faded away. Interrupted by two world wars, the capital never developed beyond a small provincial township until, in the fifties, the government established the National Capital Development Commission and generously supported its building programme.

The first decade of the new federation was marked by many changes in government for, with the exception of the Labor Party, organized political parties as we know them today did not exist, and the individual representatives therefore voted on every issue according to their personal conviction or local pressure from their electorate. Two groups apart from the Labor Party, however, emerged: the 'free traders', a politically conservative group in favour of free trade, mainly representing the interests of the wealthy land owners and sheep and cattle owners, and the 'liberal protectionists', a politically liberal group that represented local industry, manufacturers and liberal middle class.

In spite of the loose grouping the liberal protectionists, with the support of Labor, managed to form a government for most of the first ten years. The victory of the Labor Party in 1910, however, resulted in a fundamental regrouping of the political alliances. Liberal protectionists and free traders joined forces against the new common opponent, the Labor Party, and this alliance has essentially been maintained ever since, even though the names of the anti-Labor parties have changed from time to time.

Circular Quay, Sydney, in 1892.
Australian Information Service photograph by courtesy of the New South Wales Government Printer Historical Scenes

The first world war brought a strong revival of pro-British sentiments and thousands of volunteers enrolled for war service in distant, war-ridden Europe. The Australians had to pay a high price for their loyalty. At the start of the war Australia lost 10,000 men in the unsuccessful and futile attack on the heavily fortified hills of Gallipoli, and at the end of the war over 200,000 Australians had perished on the European and Turkish fronts.

Australia did not gain much from the Versailles treaty except that it was officially granted the mandate of the League of Nations for the administration of the former German colonies of New Guinea and the Bismarck Archipelago, which it had occupied at the beginning of the war. The postwar period was initially one of rapid expansion of local industry and manufacturing under the umbrella of tariff protection. Immigration from Great Britain was actively encouraged, not only to stimulate economic progress but also to populate and fill the vast country and secure it for the white race, a sentiment which repeated itself after the second world war.

The Australian economy's dependence on the export of raw materials made it highly vulnerable to any change in the economic well being of other nations. Australia therefore suffered early and heavily from the world-wide depression that started in 1929. Changes in governments at State and Federal level followed one after the other. However neither the Labor Party nor the conservative parties (National Party and Country Party) knew a solution for the world-wide economic dilemma.

The newly founded conservative United Australia Party, under J.A. Lyons, which combined the old National Party and conservative elements of the Labor Party, eventually led Australia to slow economic recovery, but the experience of widespread unemployment, combined with a surplus of foodstuff that could not be sold, made a deep and lasting impression in the minds of Australians. The maintenance of full employment has since been one of the most important political demands.

In 1939, shortly before the start of the second world war, R.G. Menzies took the leadership of the ailing United Australia Party and Prime Ministership. The outbreak of the war and the immediate Australian participation temporarily brought unity into the government benches, but after a very close election result in the following year the internal party quarrels surfaced again and Menzies was forced to resign. For a brief period the Country Party took over government but was soon replaced by the Labor Party under J. Curtin, who led Australia through the difficult war years.

The military situation at the beginning of the war looked grim. The Japanese forces had made a rapid advance and all but annihilated the British sea forces. The fall of Singapore suddenly exposed Australia to a direct attack by the Japanese, and it was obvious that Australia could not expect any assistance in the defence of its borders from the British. In a historic move, Prime Minister Curtin then appealed to the United States of America for help and his memorable speech started with the following words: 'Without any inhibitions of any kind, I make it quite clear that Australia looks to America, free of any pangs as to our traditional links of kinship with the United Kingdom'. The military situation worsened, the Japanese occupied northern New Guinea and bombed Australian coastal towns such as Darwin, Broome, and Wyndham. Gradually, however, the Japanese advance slowed down as its forces were plagued by serious supply difficulties. At the same time the American sea and air forces increased dramatically and a slow turn in the fortunes of war became evident. The combined Australian and American forces halted the Japanese advance into Papua (southern New Guinea) and slowly pushed them back over the now famous Kokoda Trail into northern New Guinea. Jungle fighting continued for months until the last Japanese were driven out of New Guinea. The immediate danger of an invasion was over and a sigh of relief could be felt through the nation. Politically this found its expression in an overwhelming election victory for J. Curtin.

Curtin died shortly before the end of the war and his successor, Chifley, led Australia through the postwar period. He was convinced that the kind of economic planning which was successful in the war period would also bring success in times of peace. The Labor programme was far-sighted and far-reaching. Particularly important was the immigration policy which, for the first time, did not restrict immigration to British sources. In the economic field the government assisted the development of a car industry and founded a national and international airline. Most important was the Snowy Mountains Hydroelectric Scheme, which was to produce two million kilowatts of electricity and supply water for an extensive irrigation scheme. In the cultural sphere, their achievement included the foundation of the Australian National University. In spite of these achievements, the popularity of the Labor Government decreased rapidly. Partly responsible for this was its stubborn maintenance of the highly unpopular petrol rationing and the sending of troops to break a coal miners' strike.

Labor lost office in 1949 and the newly founded Liberal Party under R.G. Menzies swept into the government benches with a landslide victory. Menzies was a brilliant politician and for the next seventeen years he remained undisputed leader of the Liberal Party, and held continuously the office of Prime Minister. The Menzies era was a time of general stability and continuous economic progress and prosperity. The long period of uninterrupted Liberal Party-Country Party government was made possible not only by the political skills of Menzies but also greatly aided by internal difficulties in the Labor Party and its lack of good leadership. In 1956 the Labor Party experienced a fateful split between progressive and conservative forces and the creation of a new party, the Democratic Labor Party, which drained an important number of votes away from the Australian Labor Party. It took the Australian Labor Party more than ten years to recover from this blow.

The retirement of Menzies in 1966 plunged the Liberal Party into a leadership crisis from which it still has not recovered, and the leadership changed hands five times in the following decade. This crisis, and the rise of E.G. Whitlam, a strong and articulate personality, helped the Labor Party in 1972 to end the twenty-three-year-old Liberal Party-Country Party Government. The Senate, however, remained under the control of the conservative parties, a fact which greatly restricted the new government's ability to govern.

The Labor Government started immediately, some say overhastily, to implement the reforms it had promised in its election platform. Conscription was abolished and conscientious objectors released from prison, the Chinese Government was recognized and the entire external polities were reformulated, emphasizing Australia's national interest more forcefully than before. The entire welfare programme was reformed, particularly in respect of Aborigines, migrants and other disadvantaged groups. The attitude to the export of raw materials and the foreign participation and control in the mining and exploration sector was brought into line with national interests. Conservation was recognized as a major concern for the Australian nation and the 'White Australia Policy' was finally abolished and replaced by a policy based not on race but on skills and family ties.

These reforms, however, faded away in the face of an increasing rate of inflation and unemployment. Although this was a world-wide phenomenon the government was held responsible and, certainly, its generous spending programme on welfare and education contributed to inflation. More serious politically for the Labor Government were a series of scandals which culminated in the so-called 'Loans Affair', in which the Labor Government was accused for seeking, illegally, a huge loan from Arab sources.

When, in 1975, the Senate, for the second time within two years, tried to force the government prematurely to the polls by threatening to refuse supply, Prime Minister Whitlam refused to give in and, in an unprecedented move, the Governor-General withdrew Whitlam's commission and replaced him by the then Leader of the Opposition, J.M. Fraser, who immediately called an election, which he won in a landslide victory. The Governor-General's unprecedented action and the power of the Senate, which is not strictly speaking a democratically elected house, to force the government to an election whenever it suits them has raised serious constitutional questions, the solution of which will occupy the Australian political scene for some time to come.

75 There are still areas in the remote parts of Western Australia and the Northern Territory, particularly Arnhem Land, where Aborigines adhere to their traditional life patterns. Here an Aborigine is about to take part in a ceremony, for which he has decorated his face and body with pipe clay.

76 The Ngama cave near Yuendumu in central Australia is a sacred Aboriginal site where the cave paintings – here the mythological rainbow snake – are renewed before each major ceremony.

77 Bark painting is nowadays mainly restricted to Arnhem Land and its adjacent islands. These paintings depict totemic animals, mythological ancestors or daily activities of the Aborigines and range from simple outline drawings to elaborate X-ray figures on a fully covered background.

78 These elaborately carved ceremonial spears from Bathurst Island have been covered with totemic designs and coloured seeds.

79 Carving a ceremonial spear with a hafted stone adze requires good craftmanship and a lot of patience.

80 The Aborigines of Arnhem Land acquired their skills of building dug outs from the Macassar men who visited their coasts to fish and process trepang.

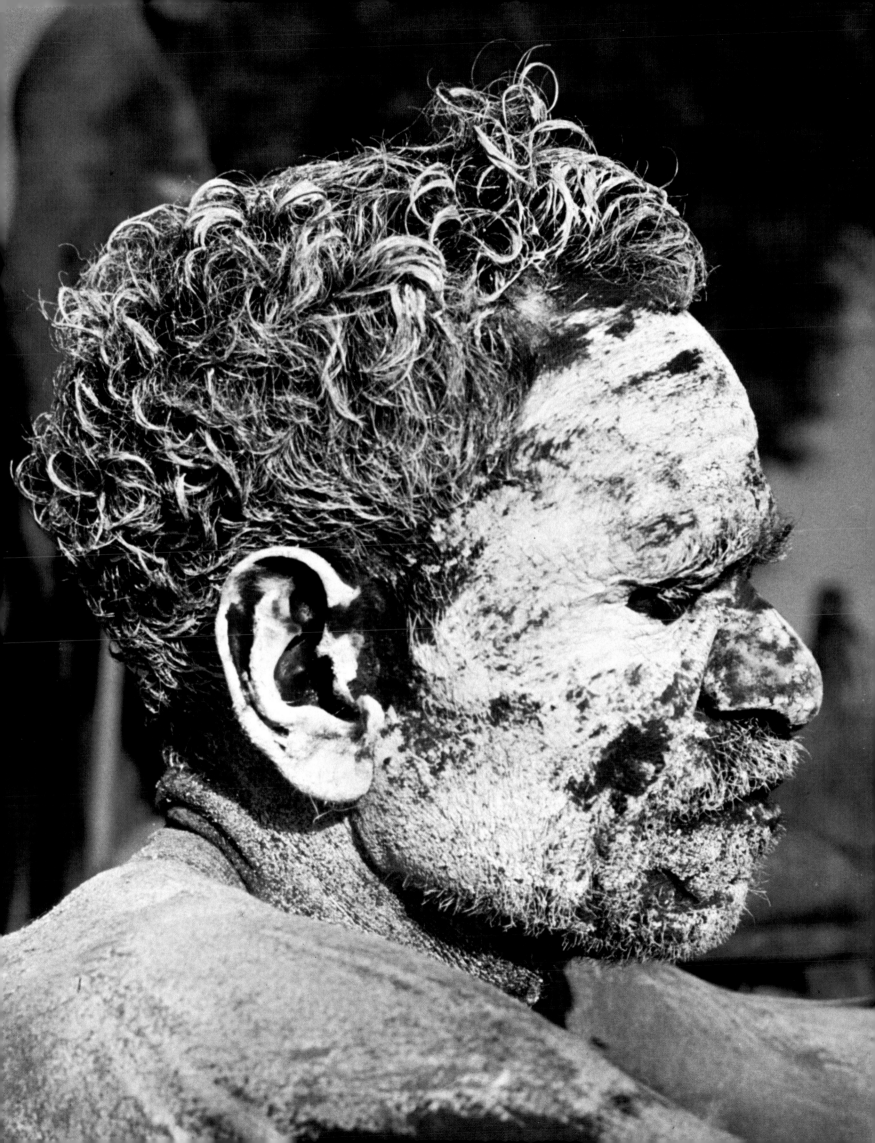

78

79 80

The Australian People

The Aborigines

The indigenous population of Australia dates back to the last ice age, when the first Aborigines migrated onto the then much larger continent. This migration started on the Asian continent, but where exactly it originated and whether it was comprised of different racial origins, is not established. Towards the end of the eighteenth century, the Aborigines all over Australia formed a racial and cultural entity. They were dark-skinned people of medium height, with wavy to curly dark hair, and their facial features were characterized by high foreheads, heavy brow ridges and deep-set brown eyes, broad cheekbones and fleshy lips and noses with wide nostrils. As they differed markedly from Melanesians or Negroes, the anthropologists named this race 'Australoids'.

Some pronounced differences in the outer appearance of Aboriginal populations in Tasmania, the coastal regions, the desert countries and rain forest areas led to anthropological speculations of various racial migrations at different periods of time. This theory is, however, no longer adhered to by most anthropologists, and it is now generally believed that such differences in physiognomy came about through adaptation to the various environments or, in the case of the densely curled hair of the Tasmanians, through natural mutation.

Before the beginning of European colonization in the late eighteenth century, about 300,000 Aborigines lived on the Australian mainland and another 5000 lived on the island of Tasmania. Probably these numbers constituted the maximum level of native population, as its size was based both on the availability of sufficient natural food resources during the worst seasons and on the carrying capacity of the women during camp-shifts. A mother could only carry one non-walking infant apart from her implements and tools. Thus sheer necessity determined this maximum population level, which had to be maintained by the Aborigines through various methods of birth control such as abstention, prolonged breast-feeding, abortion or, if necessary, infanticide straight after birth. Birth control was to the Aborigines as much a matter of survival as was finding sufficient food or water in the desert areas.

Aboriginal Society

The basis of Aboriginal society was, as in most other societies, the individual family unit. As polygamy was common all over Australia, the family unit consisted of the father, various wives – usually two or three – and their children. Before a man could take a wife, he had to pass various stages of initiation over a period of years, which actually meant that he had to reach a certain age and maturity before he could marry. Through his kinship relations within his society, his wives were chosen and betrothed to him at an early age, often when the man himself had already reached a mature age. This had a practical economic function: his future young wife would look after his well-being when his own food-procuring ability was declining with his progressive age. This situation of some young women being married to older men and the young unmarried men having to wait their turn would often cause considerable problems among group members. Infidelity was severely punished and was frequently a theme of Aboriginal legends.

A number of related families formed a local group, which was the main economic unit within Aboriginal society. Life within the group was communal and many activities undertaken by group members were planned, collective enterprises. The local group moved within a traditionally defined territory. Camp shifts were more or less frequent, depending on the seasonal food supplies, and camps were always selected near reliable water sources. Local groups contained between twenty and fifty people. This numerical restriction was once again prompted by necessity: the groups had to be mobile and small enough to avoid any rapid over-exploitation of their natural resources. During prosperous seasons a number of the tribal groups combined in larger camps. During bad seasons, however, even the small groups had to split up into their individual family units (man, his wives and children) to provide an even greater mobility, necessary to discover the few remaining food items in a large area.

The tribe was the collective unit of all groups with a common language and a common mythological background. Gatherings of all members of one tribe were rare and usually confined to the smaller tribes, as the tribal links were looked upon as spiritual bonds rather than as political units. This was to turn out as a grave disadvantage in dealings with the white settlers, where landrights issues were involved. Under white law, the tribe was not regarded as an organized political entity.

Before the arrival of the white colonists, Australia's indigenous population was divided into about 500 different tribal groupings of greatly varying size, depending on the local habitat and food supply. The smallest yet most populous tribes per territory were located in the fertile riverine and coastal regions of south-eastern Australia and the Queensland rain forests, while the numerically large population of the central Australian tribes was thinly spread over the vast arid inland.

The individual Aboriginal's position within Aboriginal society was defined by a complicated kinship system and affiliations to divisions and subdivisions of the tribe, and also by patrilineal or matrilineal heritage. Many tribes were divided into half-tribes (moieties), which were often again subdivided. Each individual became automatically part of one of these subgroups and this ensured his safe position within the social structure. At the same time, it also imposed on him a series of restrictions such as choice of marriage partners, or use of hunting and fishing territories. The observance of such restrictions and the adherance to traditional behaviour patterns was of great importance for the maintenance of order and stability in this egalitarian society which had no political leadership nor any other similar structure such as chieftains. The tribal elders exercised a certain degree of authority in respect to questions of cultural heritage or traditional tribal laws and use of the tribal territory; however, all final decisions had to be reached by consensus of all members.

There existed, however, one marked social distinction: that between men and women. It was most evident in the tradition that only men could take part in the most sacred rituals, execute ceremonial art, and know the most significant parts of tribal mythology. It was also evident in the strict labour division. Women were the main food gatherers, men were the hunters and toolmakers. At the campsites it was evident in many ways: the men would spend much of the day in their men's camp, while many of the daily chores such as collecting firewood and fetching water were done by the women.

Spiritual Culture

The existence of a rich and diverse cultural legacy of the Aboriginal people was either not recognized or was misinterpreted by early European discoverers and settlers. Only in our century is the relationship between the native view of the cosmos and its maintenance through ceremonial ritual fully understood and appreciated. In fact much of this cultural heritage has vanished with the disappearance of many Australian tribes. Our present knowledge of Aboriginal culture is based on a considerable number of anthropological studies of the surviving tribes as well as the often inadequate descriptions of former ceremonies and mythological stories of extinct tribes, and on the findings of prehistorians and archeologists who only recently began to engage in researching Australia's Aboriginal history before the coming of the white man.

The many facets of indigenous culture expressed themselves in a great variety of legends, ceremonial dances and songs and in distinct artistic styles. Yet this outward appearance of variety formed a cultural entity of the Aboriginal view of the world. The Aborigines' belief was based on the existence of two distinct worlds: the physical world around them, which was under the influence of an invisible spiritual world, called the 'dreaming', from which the physical world drew its life essence and from which it originated during the creation period, called 'dreamtime' by the Aborigines. During this dreamtime the spiritual forces inhabiting the spirit world materialized and changed the featureless and uninhabited earth into the living world. They created the landscapes, the plants and animals and the Aboriginal tribes. They divided the land into tribal territories, and gave the Aborigines their social order and laws which prescribed how the natural environment could be maintained and how Aboriginal society could be preserved through ceremonial rites and strict adherance to behavioural rules.

These laws contained detailed prescriptions for the execution of secret ceremonies, in which the creation acts themselves were to be re-enacted and presented in dances, songs and ceremonial art. Through these re-enactments the Aborigines were able to maintain the positive influence of their creator's spiritual forces on their environment and society after their return to the dreaming. Any breach of the laws would cause doom to the physical world, as the angered spiritual forces would materialize again and cause devastating natural catastrophes and other severe punishments.

Apart from these first creative beings a number of later legendary ancestors originated natural phenomena. These beings often appeared in both human and animal form and created, for example, fire, the moon, the winds, etc. They were often connected with totemism, a form of religious association, in which the Aborigines identified themselves with animals, plants and other natural phenomena. Largely the Aborigines traced their genealogy back to these ancestor figures.

Aboriginal mythology was handed down from generation to generation in a broad framework of legends, and the basic essentials of each section of the mythology were carefully preserved through very long periods of time.

Each tribe had its own complex creation mythology from which it derived its origins and the extent of its tribal territory. As the tribes were divided into a variety of local groups, these in turn would derive their particular mythological history from the creation acts that were performed within their own territory. Apart from their origins the tribes could trace every other aspect of their existence back to the events in the dreamtime, which not only helped them to define their tribal boundaries but every natural phenomenon of their cosmos: landscape features, plant and animal world, seasonal changes, droughts, floods, frosts, thunderstorms, fire, celestial bodies, etc. Any incomprehensible or supernatural features and events were explained through the influence of black magic and powerful sorcery. In most cases they could be counteracted by special ritual, counter magic or charms. In each tribal territory there were a number of sacred sites where the creative beings had performed particularly significant acts, where they had left the physical world to return to the dreaming, e.g. a waterhole, or where they had transformed their appearance into a physical feature of the landscape, e.g. a spectacular rock formation, an island, etc.

At a number of ceremonies, in which the mythological past was described and performed in a general way, all members of a cultural group, including women and children, would participate. Other ceremonies were exclusively reserved to men, like most of the initiation ceremonies, in which boys and young men were gradually introduced to the sacred aspects of their mythology and instructed in the traditional tribal laws and conventional behaviour patterns. During this educational process, which lasted for a number of years, the Aboriginal men learnt secret songs and dances, were explained the meaning of symbolic art and totemic designs and were shown the most sacred ceremonial objects, which were kept in a secret place and only used at these special occasions. The initiates also had to undergo endurance tests such as the observation of food taboos, fire ordeals or painful operations like front tooth extractions and circumcisions. Sometimes the women had their own secret rituals, which were usually related to fertility. In some areas, women were also allowed to participate in certain phases of sacred ceremonies.

Totemism formed a strong religious link between individual Aborigines and nature. During his lifetime, an Aboriginal may have had several such affiliations with totems, to which he felt a kind of kinship association. Animal and plant totems often encompassed food taboos, which may have had a significant economic function within Aboriginal society. The totems could be positively influenced by their human 'relatives' through the performance of the most sacred ceremonial rites, so-called 'increase rites', in which only fully initiated men could participate. The Aborigines believed that they could maintain the natural species through these rites, which supposedly activated the spiritual force of the totemic ancestor and guaranteed a plentiful food supply during the following season. Of a very similar nature were the rainmaking ceremonies, performed during severe droughts.

Thus the Aboriginal's concept of the cosmos penetrated every aspect of his life. He was firmly bound to his territory and his sacred sites. He had to obey traditional laws and a strict code of ethics. His totemic affiliation with nature and his concept of being an integral part of his natural environment and his tribal land, and not a conqueror of nature, prevented him from over-exploitation of his resources, and from interfering in nature's ways other than through ritual ceremony and magic. It may also have prevented major wars of conquest amongst Aboriginal tribes, as tribal boundaries were well defined by tradition and extra-tribal mythology was equally respected. To the Aboriginal's individuality and freedom it may have been a fairly restrictive belief, yet it served to maintain his society, his culture and his economy.

The Modern Population

Australia has an overall population density of two persons per square kilometre, which makes it the most sparsely populated continent in the world, equalled as a nation only by Canada. This figure, however, tells little about the distribution of the population, since large tracts of country are virtually uninhabited and the population density has to be measured in square kilometres per person rather than persons per square kilometre. The figure also completely hides the fact that Australia is one of the most urbanized nations in the world; this is not a recent condition but has been with the Australian nation virtually from the beginning of convict settlement. Of the total population which presently amounts to some fourteen million (December 1976) eighty-six per cent live in urban settlements, and nearly half of these in the two cities Sydney (2.8 million) and Melbourne (2.5 million). The great majority of the remaining urban dwellers are scattered over six cities, nearly all of which are situated close to the coast.

The most populous State is New South Wales with some five million inhabitants, followed by Victoria (3.7 million), Queensland (2.1 million), South Australia (1.3 million), Western Australia (1.2 million), Tasmania (409,000) and the two territories, Australian Capital Territory (206,000), and Northern Territory (104,000). In nearly all States more than half the population lives in the capital city. In South Australia the proportion is sixty-eight per cent, in Victoria sixty-five per cent and only in Queensland and Tasmania is the value below fifty per cent. About fourteen per cent of Australia's population is classified as rural, but even this is concentrated in a narrow strip along the east and south-west coast. The typical Australian, therefore, is not the rugged, suntanned, daring stockman or bushman as often portrayed overseas, but the urban dweller who every work day has to contend with rush-hour traffic to reach his place of employment in the city. The predominance of urbanization is reflected even more strongly in the statistics of the work force. Of the 5.2 million persons in the work force only 7.5 per cent are engaged in agricultural activities (including forestry and fisheries) and there is a steady trend to reduce this figure further.

The ethnic composition of the population clearly reflects the planned colonizing of Australia by decree of the British government, starting with the foundation of the convict settlement.

In contrast to North America, Australia has never been a haven for European immigration but remained, until the end of the second world war, a country with a population of British stock which had strong links with the mother country. This link still exists but is gradually being replaced by a stronger sentiment of national identity which is also reflected politically in Australia's increasingly independent role in world affairs.

The convict component of the present population is often over-emphasized but the time when a convict origin was a social stigma has long passed. Between 1788 and 1851 when the transport of convicts ceased (except for Western Australia where, between 1850 and 1868, 10,000 convicts were landed) a total of some 160,000 were brought to Australia. At the same time, however, over 220,000 free settlers arrived. After serving their sentence the convicts were rarely in a position to found families and the number of persons of convict origin is very small. The immigration of free settlers increased dramatically in the 1850s when gold was discovered in New South Wales and Victoria. Within a space of ten years the population nearly trebled and rose from 400,000 to 1,150,000. This surge of immigrants was of great importance for the future economic development of the country, not only because of sheer numbers but also because these settlers mostly came from a middle class background and brought with them important skills in trade and commerce and these filled an important gap in the work force and in the population composition. Among the gold diggers there were of course also people of non-British nationalities, particularly Americans and Germans who after their failures in the Californian goldfields tried their luck again in Australia; but their total numbers were small even though some were quite vocal during the events leading to the Eureka Stockade.

One important exception, however, were the Chinese, who arrived in large numbers on the Victorian goldfields in the years 1855–1857 at a time when gold finds were steadily decreasing. In 1857 the number of Chinese on the Victorian goldfields had increased to 24,000 and they represented twelve per cent of the total goldfield population. From the beginning their arrival was watched with great misgivings by the white diggers. The Chinese kept to themselves, formed closed groups, spoke hardly any English and there was very little contact or understanding between them and the Europeans. Their strange behaviour and their shy, almost subservient attitude was regarded with utmost suspicion. Although the Chinese rarely competed directly with the Europeans – they mostly worked in the spoil or in abandoned mines or pursued cheap service jobs – the whites soon developed a dislike of these foreigners who were made scapegoats for the general economic decline in the goldfields. This feeling culminated in some bloody anti-Chinese riots, but eventually subsided with the abandonment of the goldfields. However, the anti-Chinese sentiment never disappeared completely, flaring up occasionally when there was competition for jobs between whites and Chinese. Eventually it found its official seal with the so-called "White Australia Policy" (Commonwealth Immigration Restriction Act 1901) of the Federal Government. This policy, which prohibits any non-European immigration, lasted until 1973 when it was finally revoked by the then Labor Government and replaced by a non-discriminatory immigration policy. After the goldrushes, immigration to Australia slowed down markedly and the Australian-born population soon outnumbered overseas-born immigrants. At the beginning of the first world war only ten per cent of the population were born outside Australia. The total population then amounted to about 4.5 million. Amongst the immigrants from the British Isles the Irish formed a distinctive group which usually did not share the pro-English sentiments of the majority. The Irish immigrants were not only ethnically different but perhaps even more importantly they were followers of the Roman Catholic faith and usually occupied positions of low social status. The Irish group was disproportionally large amongst the convicts, and amongst the free settlers the great majority came as poor labourers who often had to fulfil long working contracts in order to pay for their voyage. The Irish element was therefore very strong in the working class and it is not surprising that the labour and trade union movement, and the Labor Party which developed from it, had a strong connection with this group and with the Catholic Church. This weakened through time but persisted for fifty years until it was broken by the split in the Labor Party and the establishment of a conservative Catholic-dominated Democratic Labor Party.

The only other major ethnic group that arrived last century and has maintained part of its identity is the group of Barossa Germans of South Australia. The original settlers came from Silesia, a province of Prussia, and they emigrated to Australia in 1838 in order to follow old-Lutheran faith which was not tolerated in their homeland. They originally settled in the vicinity of the newly founded Adelaide, but later a large proportion moved to the Barossa Valley, the wine growing potential of which had been discovered a few years earlier by a German geologist. In 1850 the first wine was produced and today the word Barossa is synonymous with excellent wines and German tradition. This German heritage has been rediscovered and revitalized since the tragic events of two world wars which led to strong anti-German feelings. Today the German tradition has become a major cultural and economic asset of the area.

The Australian population reached 7.5 million at the end of the second world war. The war, and particularly the attack of an Asiatic power on the Australian continent, not only led to a change in the political and strategic orientation and an increasing awareness of and interest in events taking place in the Asio-Pacific area, but also to a different attitude towards immigration. There was again a resurgence of the feeling that the great empty continent had to be populated and economically strengthened in order to secure it once and for all for the white race. In 1946 the Australian Government under Ben Chifley announced plans to promote and assist immigration from Europe at an unprecedented scale. The immigration was not to be restricted to British migrants but all European ethnic groups were to be welcomed. In the beginning this applied largely to the numerous refugees from eastern Europe who overcrowded the camps of the defeated and destroyed Germany, but soon it extended to other nationalities. Between 1947 and 1971 a total of 1,100,000 migrants from Europe and about the same number from Great Britain arrived in Australia. The largest ethnic group apart from the British are the Italians, who make up twenty-six per cent, followed by the Greek (eighteen per cent), Germans (ten per cent), Dutch (nine per cent) and Poles and Maltese (five per cent each). Today every fifth Australian is a non-British migrant or first or second generation descendant and nearly half of the total population stems directly or indirectly from postwar immigration.

The new migrants brought with them customs and habits which initially were regarded with considerable reservation by the Australians. With the passing of time, however, many Australians have come to appreciate that these 'New Australians' and their contribution to the Australian culture and way of life has been a major gain for Australia. The influence of Europeans is perhaps most obvious in the change of eating and drinking habits, and the great number of 'continental delicatessens' and 'continental restaurants' in every city and town speaks for itself. But also in other spheres the European influence helped to break the cultural isolation and British cultural monopoly and opened new horizons.

---

86 Much of Australia's flora is endemic which means it is unique to this country. This uniqueness is due to the long period of isolation of the Australian continent which permitted an evolution of plant and animal life without outside influences. The kangaroo paw *(Aginozanthos manglesii)* is one of these endemic plants, being restricted entirely to the southwest of Western Australia.

87 The Waratah *(Telopea preciosissima)* is the emblem flower of the State of New South Wales where it occurs in the dense undergrowth of the coastal eucalyptus forests.

88 Billy buttons *(Craspedia* ssp.) form an attractive element in the alpine flora of the Snowy Mountains where they flower in late summer.

89 Banksias belong to the family of the Proteaceae, like the Waratahs, and are common shrubs in the understorey of the coastal forests. There are over 50 species of this genus and some may grow to 10 metres in height. Shown here is *Banksia spinulosa*.

90 Some European garden flowers like this gazania have adapted well to the Australian environment.

91 Grevillea, also known as spider plant because of its long and thin stamens, is another representative of the variable family of the Proteaceae. It has become a very popular ornamental plant in suburban gardens.

92 This large flower is a Deliciosa, a member of the Araceae family.

93 *Calotropis procera* an introduced weed grows along the road verges in the arid and semi-arid zone.

94 The red salmon gum *(Eucalyptus salmonophloia)* is endemic to Western Australia but its attractive red flowers have made it a popular ornamental tree in parks and gardens throughout Australia.

95 The genus Acacia is represented by more than 700 species, more even than eucalyptus, but it is not endemic to Australia. The delicate, yellow sweetly-scented flowers make the wattle, as it is popularly known, a most attractive tree or shrub. Illustrated here is *Acacia decurrens,* the floral emblem of the Commonwealth of Australia.

96 In the dense tropical rain forest of northern Queensland, the numerous aerial roots of the ficus are an impressive sight.

97 Grass trees or 'black boys' *(Xanthorrhoea* ssp.) are a strange looking plant unique to Australia. It is quite common in the woodlands of semi-arid Australia. This photograph is from the northern Flinders Ranges.

98 The brolga *(Grus rubicanda)* seen here in flight, is one of the largest birds found in Australia. The brolgas seem to mate for life and are always seen in company of their mate. They are restricted to the northwest.

88

89

91

92

93

94

Urban and Rural Settlements

The construction of permanent settlements in Australia began only in 1788. The oldest surviving building was erected in 1794. There are no ruins of greater age, no ancient castles or city walls. When construction of the first railway began there were only 400,000 inhabitants. When the population was about half its present size of 14 million there were (in 1947) already 12 motor vehicles for every 100 people and this proportion has now risen above 45 per 100. The Australian settlement pattern is completely a product of the modern age and has been created expressly to exploit resources on a commercial basis.

The matrix of dense populations of rural subsistence cultivators that has been present throughout the modernization process in Old World countries has been entirely absent from the Australian scene. A settlement is abandoned if it proves commercially impossible to sustain production of the resources whose exploitation originally gave rise to it, and 'ghost towns' are not uncommon features of the landscape. Through much of Australia resources are so thinly spread and production costs are so high that permanent settlement has never been possible. These empty areas are mainly in the arid interior and the remote north where biological productivity is low and unreliable. For settlements to be established and maintained in any of the less favoured regions of Australia only two avenues are open. Either mineral deposits must be found in sufficient abundance to more than offset the costs of supply, production and transport, or grazing animals must be employed to harvest the sparse and erratic growth of vegetation and transform it into a concentrated and transportable product in the form of meat or wool. Through 30 per cent of Australia the costs of overcoming the environmental difficulties are so severe that settlement is precluded; through 69 per cent of the land the settlement pattern is governed in its nature and density by the character of the local resources of soil and subsoil; in the remaining one per cent are the large cities, using the resources from inland and from foreign countries, the centres of diversified production where two of every three Australians live.

Australia is a continent of a few large cities and numerous towns very much smaller in size. It is a land where rural holdings are large and where the survival of the rural settlement pattern depends on the willingness of foreign markets to receive Australian produce at economic prices. It is a pattern not fundamentally different from that prevailing in North America to the west of the 95th meridian of longitude, or throughout southeastern South America.

The rural settlement pattern contains two basic elements, the units of production themselves, which may be mine excavations or farms or pastoral properties (stations), and the clustered settlements, the townships, towns or small cities that serve the needs of the producing units. The third component of the settlement pattern, the roads, rails and communication lines, form the necessary linking element. Differing environmental conditions impose wide variations on the nature

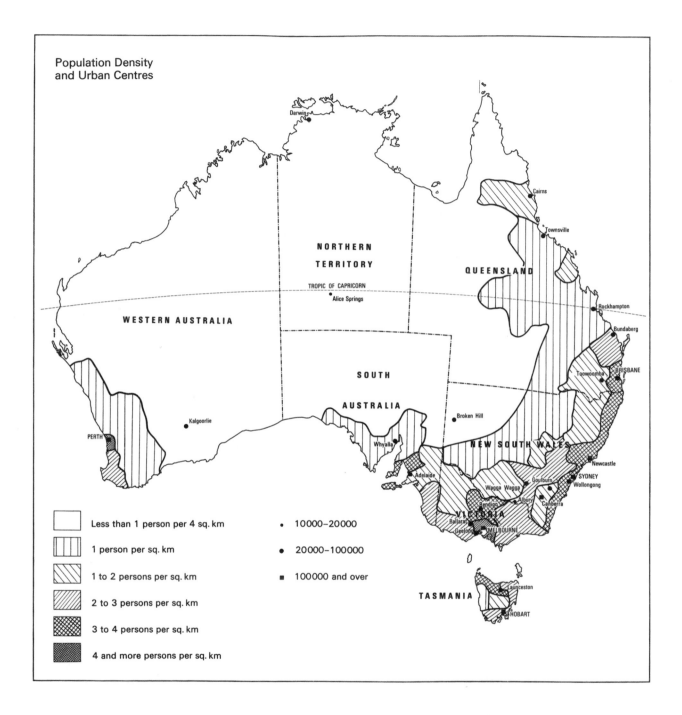

Population Density
and Urban Centres

Less than 1 person per 4 sq. km
1 person per sq. km
1 to 2 persons per sq. km
2 to 3 persons per sq. km
3 to 4 persons per sq. km
4 and more persons per sq. km

10000–20000
20000–100000
100000 and over

of the production units. Some are highly concentrated in space, like the mineral deposits, others can function only through extensive areas if they are to achieve economic viability. Notable among these latter are the pastoral units in the less productive zones, which commonly exceed 10,000 hectares. In the Northern Territory, where biological productivity is especially low, 385 units occupy 79 million ha, an average size of 206,096 ha. In the best farming areas of the south and east the average will fall to as low as 50 to 100 ha, although most properties are between 400 and 1,000 ha. In the zones of thinner pastoral occupation the distances separating homesteads commonly exceed 50 km, and the distances separating the clustered service settlements are correspondingly greater, to as much as 300–400 km. In better-settled areas distances between significant towns average around 100–150 km.

The size of the towns is directly related to the productive wealth of the areas they serve, and the complexity of the functions they perform. The great majority fall between 1,000 and 25,000 population, but where higher levels of processing occur or where there are manufacturing, shipping or regional administrative functions, the size may be greater. Such enhanced service centres are Geelong (146,000) in Victoria, Launceston (65,000) in Tasmania, and Townsville (80,000), Toowoomba (66,000) and Rockhampton (51,000) in Queensland.

There is a similarity in the design and pattern of all the service centres. Almost without exception there is a gridiron pattern of broad streets oriented to the major compass points. Land subdivision is on a generous scale with allotments averaging about 1,000 sq.m. in residential areas and the houses are set back an obligatory 6 metres from the street boundary and at least 1.5 m from both side boundaries. Houses stand individually and are built either of timber or brick, depending on availability of material, and are almost invariably roofed with corrugated iron. In some areas iron or asbestos cement sheeting may replace other materials in the walls. Along the main street buildings are larger and more substantial, with heaviest intensity of development flanking the central crossroad point. Here brick prevails and buildings are usually of two storeys. Most prominent will be the varandahed hotels, the banks, and the post office, all built in Australian styles. Their dominance may be challenged by a town hall, usually tracing its more ornate structure to European origins, and their claims to functional centrality will have to compete with a large department store, probably a branch of a state-wide or nation-wide chain. Churches, although present and prominent, are likely to stand somewhat aloof and removed from the business centre.

The physical equipment characteristic of the local economic basic activities will be important in the urban scenery, no more so than in the mining centres such as Broken Hill (NSW), Kalgoorlie (WA) and Mt Isa (Qld) and the numerous smaller settlements concerned with the extraction of coal, iron ore and bauxite. The structures of the economic base are only a degree less apparent in the concrete grain silos of the wheat belt towns, the sugar mills in the northeastern coastal settlements, the dairy plants and sometimes the wineries of the southeast, and the stockyards which are ubiquitous throughout the pastoral regions. Similarly common and essential are the facilities for trucks and rail, providing the first stages in the movement of the products of the Australian soil to the hungry mouths and mills of the world far beyond Australia's shores. These are the patterns of Australia, built first in the colonial era; but modern Australia is oriented to metropolitan development.

Ten cities, all with populations above 100,000 provide the homes for two thirds of the Australian population; the two largest of these cities contain 40 per cent of the population. Six of the 10 combine political and administrative functions with industrial and commercial activities, three are primarily industrial in emphasis, and one, Canberra, was created specifically to perform the tasks of government. Canberra (215,000) is unique in other respects. It is the only major city that is not an ocean port and it is the only one that has developed entirely within the age of the automobile (the population was only 15,000 in 1947) and designed to take advantage of the benefits offered by the car while at the same time avoiding most of the problems it creates. This the planners have achieved by compelling a widespread diffusion of employment through the unusually dispersed physical fabric of the Capital; while Canberra has been built as a garden city on the English pattern its emphasis on the automobile makes Los Angeles its nearest physical counterpart, albeit on an immensely greater scale.

99 Kalgoorlie is a mining town in the south of Western Australia and its name is nearly synonymous with mining itself. It has been in the centre of mining interest and activity since 1893 when gold was discovered, giving Western Australia its first gold rush. Together with the neighbouring mining town of Boulder, Kalgoorlie has survived the ups and downs of the mining industry and enjoyed a new boom in the late sixties with the discovery of nickel and the opening of new mines.

100–Iron ore is Australia's main mining export product
102 and the largest mines are situated in Western Australia in the Pilbara district. The ores are stripped in huge open cut mines and then transported by rail to the coast for shipment. The pictures show the various stages in the processing of iron ore. 100 depicts an iron ore train, 101 a blast furnace in a steel works and 102 the vastness of an open cut mine at Mt Newman.

103 Whyalla is one of the industrial centres of South Australia. Its main function is steel production but it also has a ship building industry which will probably have to close down soon because it cannot compete with overseas industries. The iron ore processed in Whyalla comes from the nearby mines of Iron Knob, Iron Barron and Monarch and the coal is brought in from New South Wales and Leigh Creek.

104 Port Kembla is part of the Wollongong industrial complex and one of the centres of heavy industry with iron and steel works, fertilizer plants and extensive port facilities.

105 The surroundings of Queenstown in Western Tasmania look like a desert due to the pollution caused by the copper and zinc smelters. It is difficult to imagine that the original vegetation here used to be temperate rain forest.

106 The Hume Dam is part of the extensive Snowy Mountains Hydroelectric Scheme, a system of 16 interconnected dams and 7 hydroelectric power stations that produce 4 million kilowatt of electricity and provide irrigation water for large areas in the Murray-Murrumbidgee plain.

107 Large open cut mine of Leigh Creek coal field.

108 The opal fields of Coober Pedy offer a strange sight with their numerous white mounds of the spoil of the individual mines which look like giant mole mounds from the air.

109 Desiccation crags in heavy clay soils.

110 Alumina smelter in Gladstone, Queensland. This smelter processes the bauxite from Weipa and Gove Peninsula.

111 Salt is extracted from the sea and heaped into enormous mounts at Port Hedland, Western Australia.

100 101

102

103   104

107 108

109

The other cities also display low densities, more particularly in the suburban areas that have been built to accommodate the doubling of population that has occurred since 1947; densities in their older, inner areas tend to be greater and it is these areas that many of the immigrants from overseas have found relatively attractive for residence. The general effect of low densities in creating urban sprawl is illustrated by the situation in the largest of the cities, Sydney (3,031,000), where the road distances from the central business district to the suburban extremities are daunting: 75 km along the east west axis; 94 km from northeast to southwest. A prime cause of the prevailing low density is the Australian preference for individual houses, each on its own plot of land, which is common to metropolitan and rural settlements alike. The widespread use of the car has made this form of land occupation possible and it has been further confirmed by the dispersal of industrial plants and retail facilities away from the inner areas during recent decades.

All the major cities except Canberra have significant port facilities, usually near the central business district, and with these are associated rail terminals and goods yards which contribute to relatively strong concentrations of industrial functions in the inner urban areas. In two of the cities, Newcastle (308,000) and Wollongong (202,000), both in NSW, the inner urban industrial functions are dominated by steel mills and associated metal fabrication plants which rely on iron ore brought from elsewhere in Australia to be smelted with local coal; these two cities also contribute significantly in Australia's coal export trade. The third of the large cities that is not a capital, Geelong, concentrates on automobile manufacture. In the major cities, though, the industrial structures are more diversified and less dominated by particular industries. The 5 largest cities contain 75 per cent of Australia's manufacturing industry, and for most industries their share is dominant; even in iron and steel founding and fabrication both Sydney and Melbourne far exceed Newcastle and Wollongong in the scale of their activities, although neither produces primary steel. Access to markets is the key to industrial viability, and the largest cities are themselves the largest markets, and are the locations which have the best access to any other markets which exist within the country, performing as they do the role of transport foci within their own states and between the states.

Despite the similarities in their historical experience and in their roles as connecting points between oceanic and continental transport, each of the major cities has developed its own individual character, not to be denied by the sprawling suburbs and the concentration of office employment in skyscraper buildings that they have in common. Adelaide (900,000) epitomises respectability with its trim gardens and regular streets, aspires to cultural spremacy with its biennial Festival, and justifies its indulgence in the excellent wines of its region in terms of paying respect to its early German settlers who were the first of the vignerons and who are still power-

Urban Centres, Number and Population in Groups of Various Sizes: Australia, 1966 and 1971

	Census 30 June 1966		Census 30 June 1971	
	Number of urban centres	Percentage of Australian population	Number of urban centres	Percentage of Australian population
500,000 and over	5	56.02	5	57.93
100,000–499,999	4	5.35	5	6.57
75,000– 99,999	1	0.80	..	..
50,000– 74,999	5	2.41	5	2.52
25,000– 49,999	5	1.54	12	3.20
20,000– 24,999	11	2.14	8	1.39
15,000– 19,999	17	2.47	16	2.17
10,000– 14,999	19	1.95	22	2.04
5,000– 9,999	61	3.85	66	3.66
2,500– 4,999	103	3.07	110	2.97
2,000– 2,499	50	0.96	52	0.91
1,000– 1,999	178	2.19	180	2.02
Less than 1,000(a)	27	0.16	38	0.19
Total urban population	486	82.88	519	85.57
Cumulative –				
500,000 and over	5	56.02	5	57.93
100,000 and over	9	61.37	10	64.50
75,000 and over	10	62.17	10	64.50
50,000 and over	15	64.57	15	67.01
25,000 and over	20	66.11	27	70.22
20,000 and over	31	68.25	35	71.61
15,000 and over	48	70.72	51	73.78
10,000 and over	67	72.66	73	75.82
5,000 and over	128	76.51	139	79.48
2,500 and over	231	79.57	249	82.45
2,000 and over	281	80.53	301	83.36
1,000 and over	459	82.72	481	85.38
Total urban population(b)	486	82.88	519	85.57

(a) Urban centres classified as such on grounds other than population and density.   (b) Includes urban centres of less than 1,000. *See* note (a).

NOTE. Details of urban centres, number and population not yet available from 1976 Census.

From: Pocket Compendium of Australian Statistics 1977

ful in the industry. Brisbane (958,000) quietly grows paw paws and bananas in its suburban gardens, drinks its beer as it watches the broad sweeps of the river moving down to the sea, and takes its profits calmly from the sale of real estate to newcomers escaping the colder climates of the south. Hobart (162,000) prides itself on the achievements of its sons on the football fields of Melbourne, its role as cupidity capital of the Commonwealth imparted by its casino, and on the fact that it is possible to transfer from water skis to snow skis in the space of 30 minutes. Melbourne (2,604,000) embodies the British connection, most notably among the mining companies and publishing houses, but more visibly through the prevalence of English trees and plants in its excellently maintained private and public gardens. Melbourne has both spaciousness and graciousness, is the acknowledged fashion centre for the country, has the best restaurants and the most audacious bank robbers and is fiercely jealous of Sydney. Perth (805,000) knows itself to be "the most isolated city on earth" and suspects that it is the most exploited one as well, its vitality and wealth sapped by sinister eastern interests. Perth is green trees and red tile roofs and the blue waters of the Swan River with its drifting clouds of white sails, and the keen cool wind driving in from the Indian Ocean to undercut the heat of a summer day. Sydney knows itself to be cosmopolitan and brimful of vitality, able to gather within its boundaries all and more of the waterside beauties of Perth, the ease and bounty of Brisbane, and the cultural aspirations of Adelaide. It stands less tied to Britain than Melbourne does and takes pleasure in hosting Japanese and Americans, neighbours from across the same broad Pacific Ocean that washes its golden surf beaches and sends its arms deep inland to embrace the shining city.

Aboriginal Population(a): States and Territories Census 30 June 1971

State or Territory	Males	Females	Persons
New South Wales	11,682	11,419	23,101
Victoria	2,855	2,801	5,656
Queensland	12,306	12,108	24,414
South Australia	3,697	3,443	7,140
Western Australia	11,250	10,653	21,903
Tasmania	307	268	575
Northern Territory	11,686	11,567	23,253
Australian Capital Territory	136	112	248
Australia	53,919	52,371	106,290

(a) Persons who considered themselves to be of 'Aboriginal origin'.
From: Pocket Compendium of Australian Statistics 1977

112 The Australian is an enthusiastic sportsman. He likes to participate in sport and is also a keen spectator. In the newly developed areas in the outer fringes of the cities the sporting facilites are excellent as this picture of VFL Park at Glen Waverley, east of Melbourne, shows.

113 One of the most popular games in Australia is football, in particular the 'Australian Rules' football that is widely played in Victoria. In New South Wales Rugby League is the most popular team sport.

114 Surfing draws an ever increasing number of devoted followers particularly among the teenagers. Surfing has developed into a serious sport and Australian participants have won several international events.

115 Lifesavers are an integral part of Australian beach life and hundreds of swimmers are rescued annually by these brave and much admired young men.

116 Australian coastal waters and sheltered river inlets are ideal for sailing which has become one of the most popular recreation sports. Seen here are small sailing boats against the background of the City of Perth.

117 Australian beaches are amongst the most attractive and cleanest in the world and a stay at the beach is an integral part of the Australian way of life. One of the most frequented Sydney beaches is Manly beach which is rarely seen without swimmers or surfers.

118 Aborigines have been demanding adequate land rights for a long time and it was not until 1977 that their rights were formally recognised by the federal government. This shows a demonstration for land rights in Melbourne.

119 Golf has always been a popular sport among the Australians. In marked contrast to the European situation, golf is not restricted to the wealthy but is played by anyone who enjoys it.

120 The Melbourne Cup is Australia's most glamorous horse race for which only the best horses qualify. The Melbourne Cup is televised live throughout the country and millions of dollars are outlayed on betting.

121 Holiday resorts have sprung up all along the east coast of Australia. One of the best known and most popular areas is the Gold Coast south of Brisbane which draws thousands of sun and surf hungry visitors every year. Illustrated here is the beach of Coolangatta.

122–125 The railways have been important links of the widely separated cities since last century. In Queensland the narrow gauge extends as far north as Cairns (123) and inland to Mt Isa. In Western Australia new railways are being built to transport iron ore to the coast (125). The Fremantle railway station and harbour are Western Australia's busiest facilities for the transfer of goods. The transport of people, however, has been largely taken over by the airlines and there is a dense and efficient network of flights reaching every corner of the vast Australian continent. Shown here is Tullamarine airport in Melbourne (124).

122

123

124

125

Australia – not an Asian Power

'Fear', once wrote a frank observer, 'is the *leitmotif* of Australian thinking on foreign policy' (Werner Levi, *The Fortnightly*, December 1947). Call it fear, or insecurity, or loneliness, Australians have long been conscious that their land is large, sparsely populated, vulnerable and far removed from traditional friends. Where once its 'wide open spaces' seemed an inviting target for European 'imperialists', the concern in more recent years has been the fact that it is in close, and perhaps tempting, proximity to over-populated Asia. How best to defend itself against any threats, from whatever direction they may come, has been, and will predictably remain, the motivating factor in Australia's international relations. Yet, though the goal has remained constant, the changing balance of power in the world has caused agonising reappraisals, changes in traditional alignments and practices, and now new uncertainties.

Before the second world war, Australia clung tightly to the hem of Mother Britain's skirt: until the American disaster in Vietnam, it relied on the strength and power and presence of its U.S. ally. Militarily still dependent on the United States, but conscious that its security can no longer be fully assured within the framework of the ANZUS Treaty, Australia has to chart a new and unfamiliar course without the certainty of help from great and powerful friends. Australia is not an Asian Power, as some of its politicians claim: but it is a small, though significant, Power on the Asian periphery, less suspect than the old-established Western Powers, an important source of raw materials for Japan, and a threat to none.

Its policies have not always been clear-sighted, or even consistent, and barriers do stand in the way of close Australian-Asian relations. Attitudes based on self-interest rarely win friends among neighbors, and, for many years, the preservation of a predominantly Anglo-Saxon, free, and White Australia was the objective of both major Australian political parties. Australia has lived down the stigma, but it has not attempted to become a regional leader.

Before the Japanese bombed Pearl Harbor and over-ran what was exuberantly described as the 'impregnable bastion' of Singapore, Australia did not regard itself in any way as an Asian, or Pacific, Power. Culturally, sentimentally, economically, and for the added excellent reason that the intimate association with a powerful Britain put a barrier between itself and the source of its concern about Asia, Australia was content to leave foreign affairs to Whitehall, while it counted on the strength of the British Far Eastern fleet and army, and the chain of British military bases stretching through Hong Kong, Singapore, Burma, Ceylon, India, Aden, Egypt and Gibraltar to provide for its immediate security.

By 1939, Australia had become the third largest source of supply for British needs and the second largest outlet for its exports. Whole industries and communities had grown up around the requirements of the British consumer. Even far-off Tasmania was a market garden for British housewives. Asked his nationality at this time, the average Australian could be counted on to reply 'British'. To be 'Australian' was boorish, radical and almost unpatriotic. The daughters of the well-to-do flocked 'home' to be presented at Court and to do the social rounds of the West End. They travelled aboard ships whose holds bulged with wool, wheat, fruit, meat and other agricultural produce on the journey to England, and with manufactured goods on their return. Chaperoned by their 'Mamas', this annual fishing-fleet angled for, and sometimes landed the greatly coveted British husbands, carrying them back like trophies to decorate the family sheep stations and to preserve English culture in a land in which national self-reliance was developing only slowly. Australian school-children studied British and European, but not Australian, history. Of Asia, its cultures, languages, people and history, they learned almost nothing.

In Peace and War: Loyalty to Britain

In recognition of their dependence on Britain, Australians involved themselves on a voluntary basis in everything from the Boxer Rebellion to two wars against Germany. 'When the United Kingdom is at war, Australia is at war', declared Prime Minister Menzies in 1939. His declaration was in keeping with the reality and the spirit of the time. Though Australians often found, when they met them, that they had little in common with their 'Pommie' cousins, the feeling of loyalty to Britain was deep and carefully cultivated. A handful of Australian correspondents in London reported on events there, but their primary task was to cover the world – as seen through the eyes of the British Press. Thus, the agony of France's fall in 1940 was felt almost as acutely in Melbourne as in London. Volunteers flooded the recruiting stations and went off to fight on the other side of the world under the Imperial General Staff. As a matter of fact, Australia was British, and never more proud of it.

The Pacific war brought the first of the series of profound changes. It gave great stimulus to the development of Australian secondary industries, in itself a big step toward economic independence, and it removed the British military insulation that separated Asia from Australia. Twenty days after Japanese bombs hit Pearl Harbor, and Japanese forces flowed south, invincibly it seemed, toward Australia, Mr John Curtin, who headed a Labor Government in Canberra, appealed to the United States to save the country. 'Without any inhibitions of any kind, I make it quite clear that Australia looks to America free of any pangs as to our traditional links of kinship with the United Kingdom', he said. Against strong protests from Mr

Winston Churchill, Mr Curtin withdrew the 6th and 7th Divisions, AIF, from the Middle East and turned them to the defence of New Guinea and Australia, where they served under the command of General Douglas MacArthur, the American commander in the South-West Pacific.

With the war won, many people in Australia and elsewhere hoped, and some even assumed, that the old order would be restored. Mr Churchill's declaration that he had not become Prime Minister in order to preside over the liquidation of the British Empire was echoed as late as 1949 by Mr Robert Menzies in a speech emphasizing the need for Australia to become more closely united with the British Empire. To Mr Menzies, some of the post-war changes that had occurred with revolutionary haste in Asia were abhorrent. Speaking in the House of Representatives on 15 February 1947, for instance, he attacked the Labor Government for helping the Indonesians in the struggle against the Dutch. It was, he said, 'the very ecstasy of suicide that we, a country isolated in the world, with a handful of people, with all the traditions of our race, should want to set ourselves apart by saying to our friends here and there, as in the case of the Dutch, who have been great colonists and our friends, "Out with you, we cannot support you".' Yet fourteen years later, when independent Indonesia had turned to the Soviet Union for the armaments to seize West New Guinea (West Irian), by force, if need be, Mr Menzies himself had to say to the Dutch, 'Out with you, we cannot support you.'

Radical Changes since 1949

Even after Japan had been decisively beaten, the nagging fear that its resurgence might one day again threaten Australia lingered for years. In 1949, the government of the day felt so strongly on this point that it was against selling wool to Japan, whose people faced a cold and bitter winter. It also declared a rigid non-fraternization policy for its Occupation troops, even to the point of refusing to accept the validity of legally contracted marriages. It is one measure of the changes that have occurred since 1949 that Japan by 1971 had become Australia's most important trading partner. The value of the two-way trade rose from $253 million in 1956–57 to $4,722 million in 1975–76, a nineteen-fold increase in the space of nineteen years.

To a great extent, such changes were forced on Australia by circumstances over which it had no control. When the British Empire ceased to be the world's most formidable Power, giving way to the new might of the United States and the Soviet Union, it was inevitable that Canberra should look to Washington, rather than to Whitehall, as the mainstay of its security. The faint, lingering hopes that

Britain and the Commonwealth could serve as the central force in Australia's international relationship died when Britain herself indicated that eventually she would put European unity, including political unity, before the Commonwealth and its produce.

In response to British requests, Australia in the mid-1950s contributed air support, and eventually also ground support, to the campaign to eliminate Communist insurgency in Malaya. Its forces remained there after Malaya became independent in 1957, and even after the end of the Emergency, as the war against the Communist guerrillas was called, becoming part of the predominantly British Commonwealth Strategic Reserve in South-East Asia. When the creation of Malaysia was first proposed, Canberra accepted it on British terms of reference as an orderly piece of decolonization, which, for all its initial shortcomings and potential for trouble, it indeed was. Later, when Indonesia embarked on a tub-thumping campaign to 'confront' and to destroy Malaysia, and Jakarta mobs celebrated its formation in September 1963, by burning and wrecking the British Embassy and British homes, Australia was inevitably, though reluctantly, drawn deeper into the dispute on the Malaysian side. Britain, having backed Malaysia with the intention of continuing orderly withdrawal from South-East Asia, now found herself more dangerously committed there than at any time since the end of the second world war in 1945.

The downfall of Soekarno at the end of 1965 brought confrontation to an end, hastened the British departure from South-East Asia and provided an opportunity for Australia to renew its relations with Indonesia on a much firmer basis than in the past. Relations between the two countries continued evenly and well until Australia's opposition to Indonesia's acquisition of Portuguese Timor by military force caused new frictions.

Australia's membership with New Zealand and the United States in the ANZUS Treaty in 1951 and with New Zealand, the United States, Great Britain, France, Pakistan, the Philippines and Thailand in the Manila Treaty (SEATO) in 1954, led to its active participation in the Vietnam war. 'This is not to be regarded as something that has suddenly arisen out of more recent events', Sir Robert Menzies told the House of Representatives on 29 April 1965, when he announced that the Australian Government had decided to send an infantry battalion to Vietnam. 'It is our judgment that the decision to commit a battalion in South Vietnam represents the most useful additional contribution which we can make to the defence of the region at this time. The takeover of South Vietnam would be a direct military threat to Australia and all countries of South and South-East Asia. It must be seen as part of a thrust by Communist China between the Indian and Pacific Oceans.'

The single Australian battalion in Vietnam eventually grew to a task force of three

128 129

130

131   132

133